BEFORE THE WORLD BEGAN

BEFORE THE WORLD BEGAN

The Point of the Encounter of Love and Science

Odete Martins Bigote

ISBN: 978-1-968970-26-0 (sc)
ISBN: 978-1-968970-27-7 (e)

Rev. date: 08/11/2025

Contents

Dedication

To my father from whom I learned
that hell is here, on earth.

Acknowledgments

To Ravi Chawla for encouraging me to write.
To Dr. Curtis M. Brooks and Dr. T. Peter
 Park for their long lasting friendship.
To Greg Smith for his patience with me.

Introduction

This book is my attempt to help the reader dispel fear and embrace love, which is around us, within us, and through us.

In a time of so much confusion and ignorance, we've forgotten to understand, to experience, and to share pure love; we've lost compassion.

Do you ever wonder why our preconceived ideas create models in our mind that can hurt us and cause fear, sometimes even until the end of our lives? For example, what if a family member told you that you will grow up to be fat, since your grandparents and parents were fat! Do you think this is your destiny? Do you think you have no control over this model that has been so ingrained in your mind that you cannot stop thinking about it every time you eat?

This book will show where models come from and how to change them, if necessary. And above all will show that you don't have to be scared when you hear the truth about yourself: you are a beautiful and loving human being. What happens is that we hide our beauty because of our preconceived ideas, and often we behave like monsters. We did not learn
how to handle our emotions; we are desperate, we destroy instead of rebuild.

You'll learn how to direct your deepest thoughts which you have repressed and not allowed to open up. In order to do that, you have to be confident and allow your repressed energy to show your ability to be your true self.

If Before the World Began is within your reach now, you can rest assured that you've been chosen to read it!

As to myself, I've always been curios about what is happening around me, and within me. When I started to read the Bible, I was surprised to find so many references to before the world began, and apparently no one has written about such an overwhelming subject.

Over ten years ago, I wrote You Can Remember Love:

Contemplations on Science and Spirituality. I did not realize the peace was the beginning of a new life for me, and a new way of thinking. In that book, I quote the well-known English mathematician Professor Stephen Hawking. I was enchanted by his ideas about God which he wrote in A Brief History of Time.

In 2010, when I read his most recent book, The Grand Design, I was not enchanted. I was, however, inspired to look at his writings as a mirror to what is written in the Bible. I arrived at the same conclusion of ten years ago; that before the earth was created we existed in a different from which we call spirit; therefore, Before the World Began is also inspired by the on- going war between science and spirituality.

What some scientists are writing about when referring to modern physics lead the reader to what is written in the Bible about what happened before the world began.

Do not be scared. To read this book and learn from it, the reader does not have to be a scientists, or to have read the Bible, but must willing to love and appreciate being loved, and et his thoughts flow as he answers the questions pertaining to each chapter. These questions are very important, they will help the reader remember events in their lives that they may have forgotten, but the remembrance may benefit them.

Many of us have never imagined some of the ideas presented to be possible, except in science fiction movies. However, science fiction movies are part of the dreams, uncertainties, and hallucinations.

For example, the terminology used to describe the hypothesis of parallel universes lead us to Bible's message that ours is a dreaming universe, therefore we must awake in order to return to where we were before the world began: our true home.

Parallel universe are universes that exist next to ours. They are invisible to us, they can see and communicate with us. Some physicists even call them "ghostly universes."

As you read this book you'll find out about the importance for an instant from the big bang* to the moment of our conception. You will also find out that everything is connected by an invisible energy that unites all of us and all things. And, above all, find out that you are a philosopher, even if you don't know how to read and write because you want to live a better life.

Before the World Began has many quotes from different sources including the Bible and scientists, especially physicists and mathematicians. I also include some selected articles that I wrote between 2000 and 2006. The reader must not be put off by some of the ideas and concepts presented. Please remember the fear is cast out by love. Besides, why should you fear finding out about your true self just because no one has told you about it? You must not feel embarrassed either if an intimate event that has been buried deep inside yourself begins to surface; it means you are getting help to clear your thoughts, and no one is checking you but yourself.

Fear is everywhere these days. We avoid looking into ourselves so much that we invent all forms of entertainment so that we look outside of ourselves instead of inward. Our most recent form is buttons.

Can someone investigate how many buttons we push during say, twelve hours a day? Line phones, cell phones, printers, microwaves, door bells, elevators, an infinite numbers of remote controls, computer, and so on. Is anyone interested in finding out how those buttons communicate information?

How about invisible buttons that exist within us and that we keep pushing twenty-four hours a day, even while sleeping? Well find out about the origin of these buttons, and how to handle them.

We'll discover that our uncertainties are so strong that we can never be certain of anything. Don't be disappointed because all of us feel the same way. As such, physicists are still debating whether light is a particle or a wave, or a duality. They wonder if big bang happened or not, if there were more than one big bang, or if there was one bang or many bangs. As far the speed of light is concerned, Albert Einstein taught that nothing can go faster than the speed of light which is (or was 186,000 miles per second. However, recently other scientific experiments have proved differently, but have gotten nowhere! In year 2000, Dr. Wang, Of Princeton University was able to transmit a pulse of light at a speed three hundred times faster than light! Right now, the fall of 2011, The European Organization for Research, known as CERN, and located in the Swiss- French border claim that a particle known as "neutrino" travelled faster than light and existed at creation. A few days later, they claimed that they are not sure, they explained that it needs more observation and confirmation.

We can then conclude that what we think we know today can be neither true nor real; herein lies our dream.

Be ready to learn to handle the dream and live a more peaceful life.

As you go on reading Before the World Began, you will discover that there is an observer; therefore, we are never alone.

We must appreciate this observer.

Reading and contemplating Before the World Began will help to set you free.

*Big Bang, a scientific view that the universe started billions of years ago with a violent explosion of what sometimes called a "primordial" fireball," a primeval atom," or "cosmic egg." (Encyclopedia Britannica, 1974 Micropedia Vol. II "Big Bang hypothesis.")

The Goldfish and Us

In The Grand Design, there is a picture of a gold fish inside a curved bowl. In chapter three entitled, "What Is Reality," the authors explain that a government authority in Italy strict orders to forbid goldfish from being in a curved bowl.

They claimed that placing the goldfish in a curved environment where it could see through would give the fish a distorted view of reality, and that is cruel and may even be torture. In biblical times and even before, we believed the earth was flat. In the twentieth century, we found out that the earth is not flat but curved and distorted by the mass and energy in it. Although the goldfish view is not like ours, the authors explain that the goldfish could create, and had the possibility of making scientific laws that would lead to a valid picture of reality. The authors also questions if we could possibly living inside a fish bowl and therefore have an erroneous vision of reality.

I agree that we humans live in a curved fish bowl which distorts everything, including our thinking. We don't realize where we are or what we are. We are torturing ourselves. The difference between us and the goldfish is that the goldfish was saved by a visible hand; while we know that there is an invisible hand ready to rescue us, we refuse to move.

We'll read more about this philosophical approach to the fish bowl in the chapter entitled "Spontaneous Creation." For now, let's ponder on the following quote:

> Such knowledge is too wonderful for me.
> It is high, I cannot attain it.
>
> Psalm 139:6

King David, in this quote, is exemplifying exactly what most of us are feeling right now.

Let's Rejoice.

Entertainment

We are the stuff that dreams are made on, and
Our little life is rounded with sleep.
                    Shakespeare, The Tempest, Act 4 Scene 1

Whether we believe or not, life on earth is a dream for which we find many forms of entertainment. When we watch movie, a play, or any other performance, we pay to see people acting out a script that has already been written. The story is usually fake. Many times, we do this to compensate for the harsh realities of our lives. We want to delay our return "home" therefore, we go on entertaining ourselves with all the kinds of games, until we realize that life is not a game.

Neither the performances we watch, nor our lives are real. They are based on scripts that have been written long ago, which have a beginning and an end, like Greek plays of antiquity or Shakespeare's plays from the sixteenth century. As we go on reading, we will discover that all scripts were written before the world began, including the scripts of our lives.

In the meantime please be aware that our lack of reality while here on earth is one of the emphases of this book.

Many of the ideas presented may sound like science fiction or seem very hard to accept; however, the reader should not be surprised because scientists are faced with the same problem. This means that even humans are not they seem to be. Don't be disappointed because as you go on reading, you will realize that all of us are more powerful that we can ever imagine.

There are concepts in this book that may seem new for most of us. But they can help us understand where we came from and where we are heading. Let's consider reading this book as a new form of ideas that help humanity think differently and see the truth in all of us.

Some of the ideas are repeated in different forms and with different words. Even scientists try to do that. For instance, Albert Einstein rarely mentioned the word "God," he preferred to use the idea of "Oceanic feeling".

It is not my aim to criticize theologians, scientists or anyone else. My aim is to learn, and hopefully, the reader will also learn. I am not a scientist nor I am a theologian. I am just curious, simple soul.

This book is a dialectic, which means the reader will be asked occasionally to relax and ponder, then participate and write some notes as we go along. Hopefully, we will remember events, some of which we have dismissed as unimportant. They can help us discover who we really are and that everything is connected.

Within us, there is a higher intelligence and powerful energy that provides gifts of all kinds and expects us to learn from everything and everyone. We may receive a basket full of fruit and, because we have free will, we are left alone to do with the fruit whatever we want.

Although we may think there is no need for a higher power, in moments of crisis, we often turn to it to ask for help. The problem with accepting and understanding that higher power, which has been within us since before the world began, is that, throughout history, we have given it many names such as the sun, the maker, god, gods, and finally, only one God. Unfortunately, we have not concentrated on the energy source that made the firmament, separated the waters, and much more. Now, we are ready to face the truth. The scientific advances, especially in new physics and mathematics, with its terminology, lead us to understand what have been imagined and written since the beginning of time: we are an immense invisible energy.

Many of us see God as a man who punishes us. We fear Him. We may not realize that we fear most is probably the great energy that turned chaos into order; some of us even think that it may be harmful. This happens only until we realize that the great energy is also implanted in us, and we are the real movers of the universe.

When we stop and wonder where God is, we call on him to help us, which usually happens when we are in trouble. Therefore, it is not fair to say we don't need God. I have learned in my spiritual quest that He is the creator who creates Himself by extending His energy and sharing it with us. We, in turn, create others.

As far as the basket of fruit is concerned, we may eat the contents ourselves, give it away, throw it out, do scientific research on it, and if we get mad at people, we may even decide to throw the fruit at them. These are some of the paths we can follow, just like scientists, figuring out how particles can follow different paths.

However, God is always watching how much we like to be entertained in order to delay our waking up from our dream of separation and return to Him. The choice is ours.

> Return to me, and I will return to you.
>
> Malachi 3:7

So, He goes on giving us gifts while He watches how we let our free will guide or misguide us. He knows that whatever we do, we are all working towards the same goal: to stop dreaming and return.

Therefore all things, events, and people in this universe , even the sky, were placed here as gifts for our entertainment, which sometimes can be painful.

All of us like to be entertained one way or another. We choose our forms. For instance, physicists spend their lives working with electrons and atoms, which they cannot even see. Yet what they cannot see plays a major role in our existence, and they hope to discover why we are here , how we got here , and where we are going.

The well-known professor of mathematics at the University of Cambridge, Stephen Hawking, published in 1998 a book entitled *A Brief History of Time*. Together with Leonard Mlodinow, Professor Hawking published, in 20210, another book entitled *The Grand Design*.

There is one, major, striking difference between these books. After much discussion about God in both books, Hawking ended *a Brief History of Time* by saying that if they ever discover "a complete theory of everything, it would be the ultimate triumph of human reason, for then, we'd know the mind of God." Furthermore, Hawking mentions that the discussion of the new theory should be available not just to "ordinary people, but also to all philosophers and scientists."

However, in *The Grand Design*, especially in the last pages of chapter eight, the authors explain that because there is a law like gravity, spontaneous creation of the whole universe is possible out nothing, therefore, "it is not necessary to invoke God." This is also the main emphasis of this book. What happened to Professor Hawking? Is he advancing or returning?

I will give the reader in simple terms a resume of how these authors arrived at their conclusions. I find what I am doing fascinating. I too, hope to be entertained For as long as I am needed on earth.

This time, He did not give me a basket of fruit, but a delicious soup called *The Grand Design*. This soup has so many ingredients, most of them so well-known that the more I taste it, the more entertained I am.

For a long time, mankind thought that ours was the only universe. This was agreed upon by both Descartes (1596-1650) and Newton (1642-1727). Descartes even imagined that God could not create other worlds, so say the authors. Furthermore, Descartes wrote that after God created the world, He left us alone. As time went by, we found out that there are many planets besides ours. This event must have made modern scientists very happy. They could go on punching holes in illusions like all of us. One of these hole is that there are no miracles. Both Descartes and Newton probably had no idea that they were trying to reduce God's power by imagining that God could create only our world.

As described in *The Grand Design*, chapter six (pages 136-169), something happened in 2010. NASA science teams sent to earth a photo of the sky with temperature changes dated back 13.7 billion years. They named the photo "microwave background" and concluded that such temperature changes to caused irregularities that helped gravity to form planets and us. Only the greatest of all designers, a great intelligence whish is beyond our comprehension, could make irregularities become useful regularities, among other events.

But how did it happen? The authors explain that as some areas were denser than others, gravity, which draws matter together, can cause these different areas to collapse and form galaxies, stars, our planet, and us. This event they named "spontaneous creation", which they imagine to be like the formation of bubbles of steam in boiling water. The ones that survive from the universe like ours out of nothing, but again with the help of gravity.

And the spirit of God was hovering over the face of the waters.
Genesis 1:2

We learn as we go on reading how important it is to remember that we are always being "observed".

Dear reader, please rest and ponder.

How do you feel when you remember you are not alone?

_____

_____

_____

Who is really observing you? Does it comfort you or not? Are you afraid?

_____

_____

_____

If you are afraid, what is it you are afraid of specially?

_____

_____

_____

One of the surprises of The Grand Design was the conclusion that because of gravity, the universe can be formed out of nothing.

Not at all physicists agree. People from all walks of life disagree with their conclusions. On the other hand, the authors also mention that gravity is hard to create because of the uncertainty principle, discovered in 1926 by Werner Heisenberg. It states that there are limits to measuring certain data, such as the position and velocity of a particle. In other words, when we know where a wave (light) is, we cannot know where a particle (matter) is and vice versa. Consequently, our observations produce nothing complete, only approximations or probabilities.

We may then conclude that uncertainties of all kinds are in charges of our lives. We are surrounded by illusions. Yet we choose to be here to watch the greatest show ever. We may still ask where the sky came from. What about the temperatures and gravity? What gave so much energy to this beginning universe even before we existed? Where did the energy that produced the bang at the big bang come from? Instead of giving answers, the authors mention that observations can only go as far as the big bang. They hope one day, a complete theory of everything, such as what they call M- Theory, which predicts many different universes, will answer our questions, but again without the need of God.

This is interesting because, as I already mentioned, Professor Hawking claims in his previous writings that the same theory, or as similar as one, when discovered will help us understand the mind of God.

There are Bible Commentators, such as Matthew Henry, and Keil and Delitzsch, from the eighteenth and nineteenth centuries respectively, who mention in Genesis that only God could make something out of nothing.

Chaos, to start with, was avoid and formless, and there was nothing material before the world began; only spirit existed. Matter could not have been created by God; otherwise, matter would be eternal and God creates only what is eternal.

Is the concept "out of nothing" from both science and spirituality a coincidence? Since all things are connected, and we learn this from both science and spirituality, then matter, which is neither eternal nor real, could not come from anywhere, except in a dream state made by our thoughts of separation from our eternal energy.

> The Bible reminds us of this truth.
> Wake up from your sleep.
>
> Romans 13:11

Scientists have yet to discover what they call the initial condition that produced matter. We read, however, that they have doubts about the reality of matter. Matter is not real, as we shall see. Illusions are our form of entertainment. That is the reason why there was nothing at the beginning, and chaos would have gone on forever if the spirit had not recognized the need to interfere in order to save us.

We may still ponder and ask: why do we need to be saved? Since we had free will even when not in the body form, we rebelled and started to dream of running away from the spirit. We'll read more about this event later on. We failed to ask ourselves: how can we run away from something that is inside us, like energy? As such, the great energy beyond space, time, and comprehension took care of us so that we could achieve an awakening from our dream and return to our oneness, our true self; for that reason, He provided us with two buttons that we can press to express our choices. We'll read about these buttons in another chapter. This was demonstration of His love for us.

It is true that this illusory world was made out of necessity for us to awake. It is also true that it was made out of nothing by a power that had the capacity to transform chaos into order.

It is clear, especially from reading *The Grand Design,* that matter is nothing: herein lies our dream. When the time comes, it will disappear. If the authors of *The Grand Design* intended to convince many of us that there is no need for God, a higher intelligence or energy, perhaps they will be surprised to read that their book opens our eyes to the opposite. Their wishes were transformed. I hope they will not be disappointed and that my readers will feel entertained as they continue reading.

What Happened Before the World Began?

The choice whether to take one or both paths…would have been made billions of years ago, before the earth of perhaps even our sun was formed, and yet with our observations in the laboratory we will be affecting that choice.
Stephen Hawking and Leonard Mlodinow
The Grand Design

Why and how can present observations affect choices made billions of years ago, before the earth was formed and we had a brain? Could it be that the authors know whole is in every part? All is inter-connected and independent of space and time; therefore, we do not need a brain. Furthermore, it is also clear from reading the above quote that the authors believe there was already some form of existence, in the form of energy before the world began and before we were created. When the authors mention paths, they are referring to particles. In this case, a particle is a small quantity of matter in the form of a photon which consists of light. Since we have to consider that choices were made then, the main question is who or what had the power to make the choices? This brings us to the idea of *a priori*, which means *made before* and without examination.

It had to be an extraordinary energy, not of this world, that actually understood the necessity to choose the path of light, darkness, and so on, for us to exist in this illusionary world and learn to awake. On the other hand, we must recognize that since everything is connected, the authors may be right by concluding that with observations in the lab, they affect that choice. Why observations in the lab only? Aren't human beings always observing? We also have an effect on what we observe. The energy in all of us is very powerful indeed.

The authors are amazed at the history of our world and how it maintains our stability. They realize that the process of evolution was right of our existence. As far as God is concerned, He had nothing to do with us: so, they imagine.

I concluded, especially after reading the quote at the beginning of this chapter, that *The Grand Design* is about the ongoing battle between science and spirit—between what our eyes can see and what is unseen.

I already referred to the fact that this world was made out of necessity for us to correct our mistakes of separation. Only Spirit, with His love for all of us, could have come to our rescue when there was nothing but chaos. We cannot measure love and this is a problem for scientists.

The world has to be unreal; as already mentioned, it was created out of nothing. It is based on a temporary experience, of which the real roots are invisible and started before the world began. This means, then, that ideas also existed before this world, or better yet, everything happens *a priori* in a higher plane; their information, which scientists call the initial condition, cannot be examined much less observed.

We get the same idea from reading the Bible. For example, the serpent is supposed to be fallen angel. We also read about the angels of God, called cherubims, followed by giants which were also fallen angels. They all show up at the beginning of Genesis out of the blue, so to speak. We can then conclude that good and bad angels were not created on earth, like Adam and Eve; they existed in heaven before the world began, and there they rebelled.

This is how and where the history of all of us started and ended—in heaven. This is where our models come from. In heaven, we were all one in spirit. There we decided to split; we ran away, we rebelled. We followed the fallen angels! But this idea of separation is nothing but a dream; we can never separate ourselves from our true cause. The dream is recorded in the scripts containing the history of all our thoughts about the past, present, and the future. We are not supposed to know the details of how the event started. The mystery goes on, at least for now. The details of how the event ended, we already know. But we are paying little or no attention to it, as most of us refuse to accept the accomplishment of Jesus Christ's mission as real. Jesus's mission was beautifully scripted. For that to happen, we had already misbehaved, and that means our scripts had also been written. Some scientists claim that there must be record of these events somewhere. We'll understand this concept better when we read about M-Theory and parallel universes.

The earth is the stage on which we live again, ang again what has already happened. Let us not forget that we had choices before and now. We can choose which script to follow. In this sense, we are deterministic because what we are doing is choosing again what we have already chosen. Ideas were created before we had a brain, and also our models and patterns were created. We will read about what scientists such as physicists and mathematicians, call model-dependent realism and determinism in the chapter entitled "To be or Not to Be Real."

Heaven is also where a great metamorphosis happened from peace to war—that is, from a butterfly to a caterpillar. Now we have to reverse this event.

The Bible is full of symbols to help us understand where we really come from and where we are heading. Any path we choose has already been chosen before the world began, when we were in spirit form. All of us, in unison, participated in our scripts. All of us rebelled and repented, then, our mistakes were corrected. This is why our problems have been solved, but we refuse to accept the truth. All of these events happened in an instant since time did not exist until the big bang. These ideas may seem strange and hard to accept since most of us have never even considered them. Yet they have always existed. But we should not worry; scientists have the same problems handling their ideas and principles.

We were programmed *a priori* and were given the freedom to choose. We can discover that starting with Adam. God put him to sleep, but He did not tell him the details of what he was going to do. Then, after He created Eve, He brought her to his presence, and when Adam saw her, he said:

"This is now bone of my bones and flesh of my flesh; she shall
be called Woman, because she was taken out of Man."

Genesis 2:23

It was as if he had been watching her creation while sleeping. The
script was written. The Idea had already been implanted in his mind
so that the words flew easily.

Dear reader, let's stop for a moment, relax, and ponder.

Have you ever said something and then wondered how and why?

_____

_____

_____

Did you feel sorry or satisfied?

_____

_____

_____

Did you ever go somewhere and have the sensation that you had
been there before?

_____

_____

_____
_____

Have you ever met someone and felt you had already met?

Another example is the story of Abraham and his son as written in Genesis 22. God tested Abraham by asking him to take his son and sacrifice him. The boy went without being told what was going to happen; although he questioned his father, he still obeyed.

The boy could have chosen to run away, but then history would have been different. Abraham bound his son and "laid him on the altar upon the wood" (Genesis 22:9). When he was ready to kill him, "an Angel of God called to him from Heaven" and told him to stop (Genesis 22:12). The boy knew what history had prepared for him and his family, and he chose to follow the spirit.

We have, of course, the examples of Jesus's life with many references about the fulfillment of the scriptures. An interesting example happened just as Jesus was being arrested. One of His companions wanted to fight, but Jesus did not let him and answered:

> Put your sword in it's place, for all who take the sword
> will perish by the sword. Or do you think that I cannot
> now pray to my Father, and He will provide me with
> more than twelve legions of angels? How then could the
> Scriptures be fulfilled, that it must happen thus.
>
> Matthew 26:52

In this great example, we have, again, the confirmation of the power of God and our freedom of choice, both on earth and in heaven. We will look into this quote again when we read about parallel universes.

Hawking and Mlodinow mention that what happened before the big bang "would have no observable consequences for the present." The life of Jesus is ingrained in us. Believers or not, we cannot stop remembering Him. We don't need to see Him, we just need to remember. We als0 know that Jesus is a part of history, and His short life on earth was observed by many people. Of course, we may not be able to observe what happened before the big bang, but we are always observing the consequences of such events. Everyone and everything on earth is a consequence of what happened before the world began. This concept reminds me of what I've mentioned in my previous book about what scientists call non-local reality. As you can imagine, our true reality, which is spirit, is invisible. It just is. And it is everywhere, as described in the next paragraph.

Scientists call this reality non-local. In 1982, mathematician John S. Bell's proposal, known as Bell's theorem, and the experiment of physicist Allen Aspect proved that there is a non-local reality. However, it is interesting to notice that Bell proposed that a local reality exists between particles, while Aspect proved the opposite. Non-local shows that distance does not matter, and there is a communication that is usually invisible and everywhere. This communication is independent of space and time, and it is part of parallel universes, as we shall see.

It should be no surprise that all of us have the freedom to choose what was written before the world began; then we come to earth to experience our choices. When we encounter someone, whether we like it or not, we may discover that we are engaging in non-local relationship. There is an invisible communication uniting us and hopefully helping us realize that we are all mirrors to each other. We all come from the same cell.

The Bible commentators Keil and Delitzsch mention, "Even Satan was created as a good spirit of God, but he abused his freedom and rebelled." Satan too had a choice. Let's hope one day we'll learn the details of this event. We'll learn that the dream of separation from our source can never splits. There is an atom in every cell that never dies.

Furthermore, as we know, the story of Jesus was prophesized for centuries, long before He appeared on earth. From reading the Bible, we learn that He always existed:

He was in the world, and though the world was done
through him, the world did not recognize him.

John 1:10

At the right time, He showed up in physical form. Why not before? Here, we also get the idea of what happened before we were in the body form. As already mentioned, a rebellion against our unified energy started; in other words, we sinned. But it took mankind thousands of years to be prepared for His arrival. All was very well programmed far in advance and continues to be so.

Thousands of years ago, mankind was not ready to imagine what could have happened before we existed. They had no idea of the beginning of our planet. The theory of the big bang was not discovered until the twentieth century. Now, the time has arrived for us to accept these events.

I also stand by what I have written in *You Can Remember Love* (Bigote 2000) over a decade ago that "the physical world is an illusion that we made and collectively sustain." We thought we could create by ourselves and, therefore, separate from our eternal energy. This is the reason why it was chaotic to start with.

Without Me you can do nothing.

John 15:5

Only a rebellious nothingness, Malignant entity, could have a dream of trying to make a split and create chaos out of spirit. Chaos was a nothingness.

But Spirit started to hover above the chaos and began to create earth, heaven, and all living creatures. Then, He gave us the freedom to make choices and apparently left us alone. This event of creation is no illusion. What is illusion is the mask we built to cover Spirit, our true self.

The truth is that Spirit never left us alone. It is in us. It is us. Just because we cannot see it does not mean it does not exist and have influence on us. Even scientists believe in what they cannot see, like electrons and atoms; yet because they work with them, they must have some faith in them and consider them useful. We refuse to face and accept the simplicity of life; we choose to be entertained by complicating it with our game playing.

Think well, folks. Scientist say that time started at the big bang when the universe was a small as the Planck size, a billion-trillion-trillionth of a centimeter, and kept expanding, thanks to gravity. However, some scientists have doubts about gravity, as what we've read.

Dear reader: Please rest and ponder.

Do you believe only in what you can see?

_____

_____

_____

Do you believe the size of the universe at the big bang as small as mentioned above? If so, can you imagine how small you were, say, at third week of conception?

_____

_____

_____

Does size and measurements have anything to do with what goes on in the mind and beyond?

_____

_____

_____

What about our feelings: where did hate, envy, false love, anger and so on, come from? They could come only from fear of that great intelligence and energy from which we started to run away long, long ago, and continue to do so.

Many of us still think we are not believers. Think well, we must believe in a power superior to ours. As a matter of fact, our belief is so strong that we don't stop being afraid of being punished. So, the truth is that it is not God, the man, we are afraid of, but of His energy. Because if we don't believe in His powerful energy, why are we running away from Him?

We don't even realize how much damage we are causing to ourselves by limiting our knowledge. We have not learned to handle our emotions. We continue to observe, without realizing, or even appreciate that we are being observed.

Just before his arrest, Jesus prayed for his disciples. I'll go even further and say that He prayed for all of us.

Father, I desire that they also who You gave Me may be with Me where I am, that they may behold My glory which You have given Me; for You loved Me before the foundation of the world.

John 17:24

In this quote, we learn again that everything has already happened before the world began and ended in glory. Our problems have been solved, as I already mentioned. The life of Jesus is the major event that happened before the creation of the earth. So why worry?

Dear reader, please rest and ponder.

What are your thoughts about this quote?

_____

_____

_____

Do you realize that you, too, existed before the foundation of the world? Or do you need to go on reading before you can respond to this question?

_____

_____

_____

Jesus came to earth not just in spirit but also in bodily form to help us wake up. All events that we think are happening now, either individually or collectively, have already happened. Before creation, Jesus died because of our mistakes, otherwise known as sins. If we had not sinned, Jesus would have no need to be created and to die for us. If we had not made mistakes, we would have no need to be on earth. It is true that we make history; we are the creators for better or for worse. We created a dream of separation. But we know our real creator is within us.

For God saved us called us to live a holy life, He did not because we deserved it, but because it was His plan from before the beginning of time- to show us His grace through Jesus Christ. 2 Timothy 1:9

We still choose to continue to observe what we see, instead of believing and admiring what we cannot see. We forgot what the earth was offering from us from the beginning- its minerals, food, abundance of all kinds of place here by someone who knew of our needs in advance. We allow ourselves to be poor in spirit, indeed. Hopefully, one day, we will be transformed.

To Be or Not to Be Real

According to the idea of model-dependent realism…our
brains interpret the input from our sensory organs by making
a model of the outside world. We form mental concepts of
our homes, trees, other people, the electricity that flows
from wall sockets, atoms, molecules, and other universes.
These mental concepts are the only reality we can know.
-Stephen Hawking and Leonard Mlodinow,
The Grand Design 6

To help us understand model-dependent realism, the authors use the work of mathematician John Conway, dated 1970, called the game of life. It is based on present observations and the mental models we make, which sometimes make us unaware of their influence in our lives. The authors hope it will explain why we behave the way we do and will help us think about reality and creation.

Conway imagines little square blocks like a chessboard, which expands infinitely. He concludes that ours is a deterministic universe. This means he believes that we are not free to choose, and we are ruled by causes independent of our will. He completely dismisses the fact that our will and God's can only be one and the same. Whatever has been determined is in accordance with our will, which was written before the foundation of the world and is lived on earth.

As already quoted above, Conway also explains that our brains "interpret the input from our sensory organs" and make models of our outside world. How about before we had brain? A tiny fetus in the womb moves often. It sucks its fingers and moves its legs, arms, and do forth. Who or what is touching its brain before it is born, or better yet, what is the fetus looking at? We'll read about this question in the chapter titled "Spontaneous Creation."

In the Bible, we have the example of John the Baptist, who "leaped…

for joy" in his mother's womb (Luke 1:41, 44) when Mary, Jesus's mother, arrived. John acknowledged the birth of the Messiah before both of them were born. John had no eyes but he could see. He could see eternally. He had no heart, yet he could express joy and love eternally.

According to Conway and his square blocks experiment, the brain obeys scientific law as they "generate generation after generation." He also concluded that the blocks are intelligent and self-replicate.

Hawking and Mladinow say that such models are what we use in our daily lives. I envision that these models were built in our mind before we were born and had a brain. The Bible also confirms this truth, as we read in the above quote about John the Baptist, and there are certainly many more examples of this.

Our brain is a temporary machine. We are not temporary; we are eternal. I guess scientists want us to think., again, and again, that we don't have a brain, we stop existing.

As described in chapter three of The Grand Design, "model-dependent realism corresponds to the way we perceive objects." It is clear that it does not relate to our real past, that it is, to our origins-our initial condition before the big bang. Scientists do not have the mathematical knowledge to go that far. How can this be? Past and future are connected like everything else. Model-dependent because it makes us believe in a reality that does not exist- the outside world.

Let me share with you an event that has to do with my help. My mother was always complaining about her thyroid and protected her neck, especially with scarves. She even asked the whole family to place a scarf on her when she died. Unfortunately, I arrived just a few hours before the funeral and my aunt had placed the ugliest scarf we had on her.

For many years, I remember that either consciously, I too liked to protect my neck and used scarves of all kinds. It is true my mother had become my model. One day, my doctor told me I had a thyroid problem. Immediately I asked myself if it could have been inherited from my mother.

There was no way I could check if the other generations had thyroid problems. And neither can I check the origin of the problem which must have happened eons ago. I was, however, obsessed with the idea of model-dependent realism. What is important to remember is that everything we do is connected to a distant past is our true and ultimate reality. What is happening now is chosen to go through, the roots of which are a mystery. We will read more about models in the chapter title "Models and Patterns."

Please relax and ponder.

For now, can you think of any event in your life when, either consciously or unconsciously, you remembered something that happened in the past and had a consequence in the future? How did it influence your life?

Have you ever imagined an event, and then you see it materializing when you least expect? Were you surprised?

Scientists like all of us, struggle with the concept of reality. We used to imagine that by direct observation we could obtain knowledge of the world. We thought that we saw externally was real. For example, if we watch the sun rise in the morning and set in the evening, we assume it is real.

But, as mentioned in chapter two of The Grand Design, modern scientists provide us with another approach. At first, they conclude that our thoughts about the reality of the sun are a reflection of "an external reality that exists independent of the observer who sees it" In other word, they imagine there is another observer observing us. They think it is external because they insist on giving reality to what is physical.

In the book entitled *The Universe and Dr. Einstein*, it is written that philosophers and scientists have concluded that, "since qualities exist only in the mind, the whole objective universe of matter and energy, atoms and stars, does not exist except as a construction of the consciousness, an edifice of conventional symbols shaped by the senses of man.

We can then conclude that only the consciousness of the authors of *The Grand Design* are reminding them that there is another observer observing us. This is a true discovery because our observation is fake, compared to the true observer who is unchanging and within all of us. Consequently, what we observe in time and space is illusion, which is exactly what Albert Einstein discovered. Nothing in this world really exists except the spirit in us which is eternal and makes us move.

In the meantime, the idea of an external reality independent of the observer must continue to be a mystery and a difficult concept for scientists, which they hope to solve with the upcoming M-Theory.

But going back to chapter two of *The Grand Design*, the authors end up wondering if "we have any reason to believe that an objective reality exists." They refer to the sun, the moon, and so on.

This very interesting question is a reminder of Revelation, the last chapter of the New Testament, which causes a lot of stress in most of us. Why does Revelation cause us stress? It is because of preconceived ideas that we have built in our minds which lead to wrong models, for instance: could it be that we have been told this earth and life here is real and is all there is? We read   in Revelation 8:12 that the power of the sun, moon, and stars were "reduced." Could it be we do not realize the same power is in us? In the end, when everything and everyone is transformed, we do not need the light from the sun, the moon, and so on because we will then realize that we are the light. Could it be we do not realize God is in charge of all events within us and outside of us? As it is written Revelation 21, all illusions and uncertainties "will pass away" and "all things [will be] made new." This is transformation. Some of us may even call these events "miracles." The authors of *The Grand Design* claim that there are no miracles.

But miracles are, in the end, very natural because it is our initial condition to which we are returning to. Miracles are always happening. This book describes many miracles, and the fact that I am able to write it is a miracle.

Still, while we are on earth, our entertainment goes on, as we continue with our game playing. Do scientists specify where our real thoughts started from? They cannot. They are prevented from doing that; so far they are not allowed to dissect what happened before big bang, consequently, they claim everything started at the big bang, and our brain obeys scientific laws, because that is what they are allowed to examine. Even so how can they be so certain, if everything is uncertain? Remember the uncertainty principle that was described in the second chapter. It specifies that our observations produce nothing complete, only approximations and probabilities.

Furthermore, how did they arrive at the conclusions that the universe is deterministic? They believe that "once you set up a starting configuration, or initial condition, the laws determine what happens in the future."

First of all, as already mentioned, scientists can never know what our "initial condition" really was; we understand that they are basing their research on what happened after the big bang and cannot dissect what happened before. This is why all their principles and theories can only be incomplete. However, as they research M-Theory and parallel universes, they are just beginning to scratch the surface of what happened just before big bang. They believe that parallel universes existed with or without big bang! We'll read about this on more detail in another chapter.

Our initial condition could originate only from beyond this world, beyond our understanding while we are here on earth.

In the end, as already mentioned in this book, it is true that we, like the universe, are predetermined. The Bible teaches that God is involved in everything:

In Him also we obtained and inheritance, being
predestined according to the purpose of Him who works
all things according to the counsel of His will."

Ephesians 1:11

However, we have free will to choose which path to follow among the paths that we have already chosen. This concept may nit seem real, but it is real within our illusions in space and time. We may imagine the paths to be science fiction, but what we call science fiction comes from parallel universes: is there anything new under the sun?

We know where those laws that determine the future come from. WE also know where the script comes from. We are not interested in doing any investigation: we are interested in experiencing life on earth. If scientists choose not to see life this way, that is their choice.

But they still question if we have free will or not, and say nothing about love and hate. At first, Hawking and Mlodinow tell us that free will is an illusion. Later on, they change their minds. They realize that complex beings like us have trillions of molecules and other particles that make it impossible for scientists to predict our actions, not to mention that fact that we have choices.

We can see how much our Maker limits the power of scientists to study us by making our bodies so beautifully complex that they cannot be

Thoroughly dissected and investigated. We are also ideas, which, like the spirit, stay always connected to their source.

In my previous publications I give the example of a chair and how my thoughts, and therefore pre-conceived ideas, influenced the way I saw the chair. However, I did not realize that those ideas could have come from eons ago, and that I had created what modern scientists call a model-dependent realism. It is ironic that some of the theories scientists present such as speed of light, non-local communication, and parallel universes, can help us understand our real source and that we are learning to return to it.

The creation of all events cannot be thoroughly examined and dissected because they come from a realm that is beyond space and time. This is the mystery of life.

In accordance with modern science, I would like to add another aspect of looking at the chair, which can be any other or even people. The moment we observe something, the light—that is, the energy from us—communicates with the light from whatever it is we are observing. This event lasts only an instant. In other words, what we see, for instance, in a chair, is just its light mingling with our light. Then, we make images, and in this sense we are the creators as is mentioned in *The Grand Design*.

In the meantime, we limit and disturb what we are observing while at the same time, the observer and observed become unified. In us lies the power of spirit, as we saw in the example of the chair.

Physicists continue to question the reality of the chair even if we are not observing it. In the end, the chair may not even exist at all, so they used to think. But now, they seem to change their minds. Why? I believe because of their research of the M-Theory, which leads to parallel universes as we shall see later. This way of thinking may seem new and weird to most of us. However, such thoughts have always existed in may people's minds, especially in the minds of modern physicists and mathematicians who feel frustrated by their theories and hypothesis, which once properly discovered, they hope will show that the universe created itself and, therefore, does not need God. This is the theme of *The Grand Design*.

Dear reader, please rest and ponder.

Have you ever seen science fiction movies? What was your reaction? How did you handle it?

_____

_____

_____

Do you realize that your life could be seen as a science fiction movie by people who live in parts of the world completely isolated from ours? Have your thoughts about science fiction changed, then?

_____

_____

_____

How do you feel reading about predestination and that we still have choices?

_____

_____

_____

Physicists also question if we can assign reality to what we cannot see. Those of us who believe in a higher self can, but what about those of us who do not believe?

This is an interesting question because, as referred to throughout this book, physicists often work with electrons, quarks, and other particles which they cannot see. They must believe in them or at least have some faith; otherwise they would not spend their lives working with what is unseen.

In *The Grand Design,* we read about Edwin Hubble. In 1992, he concluded from his observations of galaxies that the universe is expanding. But he could not see the expansion. Neither could he see the galaxies; he could only observe the light from them.

> By faith we understand that the worlds were framed
> by the word of God, so that the things which are seen
> were not made of things which are visible.
>
> Hebrews 11:3

In this quote, the Bible confirms that we cannot see our original condition. We cannot see where and how our scripts were written.

All we are doing is entertaining ourselves by trying to make our dreams look real while scientists keep investigating. They cannot get rid of that great ghost in the back of their minds, which they call the uncertainty principle.

Physicists are very aware that, in spite of their hard work, they cannot be certain of any of their theories. This means they must believe, or at least hope that certainty must exist somewhere else other than the earth.

All of us like to keep digging holes in illusions. That is why I mention that life is an entertainment. Our lives are full of uncertainties. Even the latest scientific theories are uncertain. Consequently, if we question reality and certainty, where does that lead us? It can only be that we are all dreaming, and that ours is a dreaming universe.

I Dream --- Fathomless
I dream --- fathomless, endless.
I sleep --- useless and issueless.

God sleeps --- the world this is.
But if I also could
Sleep a sleep like God's
I might dream the Good---
The Good of the [1] I exist.
That dream, I glimpse in the distance,
In me I call Christ.

-Fernando Pessoa, "I dream--- Fathomless"

For centuries, other cultures such as Upanishads (1500 to 600 BC) claimed that the worlds was an illusion. They went further to say that the spirit is the highest perfection.

How can we ever succeed in making laws to govern our illusions? We fear the great intelligence and energy so much that we try to make chaos seem real and eternal.

We must remember that the Spirit of God is always observing us. We cannot observe spirit, just imagine and pray while Spirit observes us.

That great energy beyond earthly sciences is spirit; this is the only reality there is. It is eternal, it never changes, and for us and in everything. Our world was created all other worlds.

Hawking and Mlodinow mention that it takes work to separate the earth and the moon. Only an energy beyond our understanding could have achieved that great accomplishment. For God nothing is impossible.

Albert Einstein taught that our wholeness is shared. It has been extended to us here on earth since creation, and we extend it to our creations. It is through us that this is done. We are very powerful indeed. We are needed on earth, in spite of dreaming.

And the Lord God caused a deep sleep
to fall on Adam, and he slept.

Genesis 2:21

Is Adam still sleeping? Are all of us sleeping? How about dreaming?

Where Are the Birds?

I once watched a flock of birds performing a perfect spiral dance, They built two nests on the façade of the building across the street from where I was. I don't know what they were celebrating, but they were certainly flying in what seemed a joyous formation. As they chirped, each of them took their turn flying very close towards the nests but wouldn't touch them. They never stopped and continued to fly high over the roof of the building only to come back again to circle the nests as closely as possible. There was unity and harmony in their spiral dance, which lasted quite a while.

I was flabbergasted. I asked God not to stop them and to take care of them. I wanted to go on contemplating their performance more than anything else in the world. In the Bible, there are many references to birds and the importance of bird watching as we read in the following quote:

> Look at the birds of the air, for they neither sow
> Nore reap nor gather into barns; yet your heavenly
> Father feeds them. Are you not of more value that they are?
> Matthew 6:26

I did not have to ask God to take care of the birds. He does that always. He takes care of everything, including us.

More than once, I noticed one bird going inside the nest. It was not participating in the spiral dance and showed up flying from somewhere. Then it came out a little later and flew away again. Only once, I saw a bird being followed by another, and both went inside the nest. Soon, they came out and flew away too. They disappeared very quickly. While all of this was going on, the spiral dance and chirping never stopped.

What were those two birds doing inside the nests? How could they fit in such a small space, especially if they had eggs inside? What were they celebrating? Birth? Mating?

Later on, I found out that they were swallows. Their nests are made out of mud, which they themselves carry on their beak and pile until it hardens. The nests last many years. Their location is carefully chosen, and built in protected areas high enough so that no one disturbs them. They can be built on the façade of concrete buildings or wood. When the babies grow up, they too build their nests next to theirs.

I knew I was watching a nature at work with an invisible intelligence guiding the birds. We can call that intelligence connection, correlation, non-local communication, and so forth. In the end, there is no need for words; they don't even matter.

It is true, we have in this book and everywhere examples of what scientists call non local communication. We will read more about this type of communication that always existed between all things and everyone—between myself and my father, between the sheep and the shepherd, between the little lambs and their mommies, between scientists and lay-people, and, of course, between birds and us.

But, eventually the birds disappeared. "where are the birds?" I said out loud. Complete silence followed. Then, my inner voice told me, "The birds are within you."

Rest and Ponder:

Have you ever watched nature manifesting this way?

_____

_____

_____

Do you still wonder who is in charge of all of us?

_____

_____

_____

Models and Patterns

Years ago, I thought I was in love with a handsome man, but I could not date him because he reminded me of Paul, whom I had met before at Columbia University in New York City. One day, I thought Paul was going to kiss me, but instead he bit my nose.

We are influenced by our preconceived ideas. We make patters that may show themselves for the rest of our lives and beyond. Such patterns determine what happens in the future. Our dreams depend on them. The main questions are how and where are the patterns made? In other words, what is their initial condition? As a consequence of what I read in *The Grand Design*, I envision that what happened with Paul had become what the other authors call model-dependent realism, which was presented in the chapter titled " To be or Not to Be Real."

I imagine that if I could dig deeply into my encounter with Paul and go back in time, I could go through generations upon generations, billions of years of similar events. Therefore, since all is connected, this long journey would lead to my nose being mistreated in some other forms and maybe even on other universe. This looks like science fiction.

We know from our life experiences that we create patterns which lead to events repeating themselves sometimes in an unpleasant manner. But we are beginning to realize that such patterns originated before the world began. Everyone we meet already had an encounter with us, even for an instant. Modern science is showing us how these patterns are formed, but they claim the brain plays a major role as we have read. However, others claim that the patterns were created not only before we had a brain but also before we had a body as we read in other chapters.

What we are doing while on earth is living again and again what has already happened. Everything comes from the past, that is, what happened eons ago, not from what we are observing now. But because we are dreaming, we think it is now. Plato taught that we have forgotten everything. Now we need to go through the same experiences in order to remember.

Rest. Ponder. Try and remember and event in your life that has already happened before—one in which you were very aware of the details. You may even be shocked. You ask yourself, "how can this happen again?" or even, "why is this happening?"

_____

_____

_____

Do you ever feel that you are following a pattern that has been ingrained in your mind and is not helping you?

_____

_____

_____

Did you wish to change that pattern? If so, what did you do to change it?

_____

_____

_____

If you did not wish to change, can you think of the reason?

I recall several examples in my life and with my friends that I'd like to share with you. For instance, I remember dating three men. All of them were alcoholics. Two of them were in AA, and one was drinking heavily while dating me, but not in my presence. At that time, I was not aware that patterns have consequences. Of course, we cannot go back to the events before the world began, but I still asked my family if they remembered any past history of alcoholics, and they did not.

I have no idea why this happened. However, while dating one of them, I started to drink more than ever. I was lucky and got drunk only once. Then I went back drinking very little.

Another pattern was made when my boyfriend told me that he could not fly because he suffered from claustrophobia. I prayed and eventually let go of the boyfriend and suffering.

But, perhaps, the greatest of all examples is the story of Catarina, a friend of my family. She was a dressmaker and made a lot of money. She was married to a man who frequently abuse her. In spite of everyone's advice that she should divorce him, she chose to live with him until she died.

Catarina's love for her husband was an example of unconditional love, and forgiveness. It was also an example of following a pattern of abuse, misery, and unhappiness. She chose not to change her pattern.

What happened to her husband after her death? He lived for years in complete misery. He was stressed and very lonely. Here is a great example of how the ego works in our lives—love and hate. Here is also an example of someone who followed the patterns he got used to: misery, unhappiness, and even abuse—what he did to his wife, he did to himself. He too chose not to change patterns.

This does not mean that all our patterns end up the same way. Neither does it mean that they are all bad. It all depends on the mysterious circumstances that we cannot observe now, as well as our faith and choices.

Years ago, when I used to go swimming in Manhattan, I met a woman who always caught my attention. She seemed very relaxed and loved to wear a lot of jewelry, even while swimming. One day, another woman approached her and greeted her. I realized that they used to be friends. Then, the woman I knew turned to me and, in a very low voice, said, "I never want my friends to know where I am. I have no idea how this one got here today. They all know that I marry only millionaires. The last one died six months ago. I am about to marry another one who lives in my building. They are all so curious. They want to know as much as they can about me." In the end, she concentrated mainly on one event—making patterns with millionaires. She was probably afraid that her friends might steal her rich boyfriends from her.

How about animals? Do they have models and create patterns? I believe they do, as you can read in the following story. It was always a pleasure to visit Ann and Martin. But that was only until the day they decided to bring along their quite dog in their car and drive me to the station. Ann was driving, Martin was sitting next to her, and the dog was in the middle. I was sitting in the back behind her. In those days, there were no seat-belts. As soon as she started to drive out of her driveway, I noticed the dog was getting very excited. Then, to my great surprise, with just a gesture from her, the dog sat on her lap, while Martin begged her to give to dog back to him.

In the meantime, the dog had his paws on the wheel; he was looking straight ahead and diligently observing the road ahead of him. Martin insisted on taking the dog from her lap, but to no avail. Instead, she laughed and raised her arms up in the air a few times, while the dog kept his paws on the wheel and gently moved it.

The dog was driving, and I was shaking with fear. Although it was only three miles to the train station, this time seemed like the longest car ride of my life. It was also the most interesting. Ann told me that the dog's behavior was consequence of him watching her driving. "The dog got used to my style," she said. "I just trained him to sit on my lap and place his paws on the wheel."

I have learned from this experience that animals, like us, have their models. Based on their emotions, love, anger, and, so on, they observe and imitate. They too create patterns, but unlike us, they probably do not seem to care where the patterns come from and how they are formed. I wonder if dogs know anything about events before the world began.

If we can see the events in our lives this way, we may begin to understand that not only is everything connected, but also that we would eventually end up where it all started; that is, before the world began, before the big bang, when our brains did not even exist. We have read that what scientists call model-dependent realism was created before the world began; consequently, I believe what happened in ll the examples I mentioned was based not just on what I experience at that time, but on experiences of a long time ago. The source of what happens now while we are here on earth comes from before we existed as we have already read. There is a need to take action to correct some events that produced thoughts in our mind. That experience has already been designed for us, and its origins may remain a mystery for as long as we are on earth. Jesus had to take action often, in order to accomplish what was predestined.

When Jesus started to described to his disciples what was going to happen to him, such as being arrested and crucified, Peter called him aside and said,

"Far be it from you Lord; this shall happen to
You." But Jesus turned to Peter and said, "Get
Behind me, Satan. You are an offense to me, for
You are not mindful of the things of God, but
The things of men."

Matthew 16:22, 23

In this quote, Jesus is answering Satan directly. Satan did not want the scriptures to be fulfilled and used Peter to express his wishes. As far as modern science is concerned, Jesus could have just as well told Satan that he was not following the model-dependent realism that had been created millions or even billion years before by His Father. Such a concept would not have been understood at that time.

As well all know, Jesus made history by letting himself be crucified. This model-dependent realism became a pattern for many of us, believers or not, because we keep crucifying ourselves too often. We do not realize that we are all navigating on the same boat with an invisible captain. Prophesies described in scriptures became our models, which manifest in parallel universes as well as we shall see.

Many times, when something happens in our lives that does not make us happy, we tend to say, "This is my cross." Princess Diana mentioned in an interview that her marriage to Prince Charles had been her cross.

In truth, we know that our true reality, our essence, is created by the spirit—that great energy within everything which is beyond measure and observation. The problem is that we keep looking for causes and solutions apart from spirit. We forget that all things, events, and the people we meet are a reflection of our inner self and our needs; this is no illusion.

We may pray and ask to heal. This means that since we have built that type of model-dependent realism a long time ago, we bring the healing model to view and, of course, that great energy within us may eventually heal us.

But how? Let's remember what we forget often, even in accordance with modern science—that everything is connected. Albert Einstein found that out, as we'll read in the chapter entitled "Science and Philosophy." Consequently, since everything is connected, it all started before the world began, before science as we know it. It all started *a priori* with spirit as we now understand.

Fear must have been among the first models made because it was the fear of God's energy that caused our dream of separation. We could have chosen a different model, such as seeing ourselves as one with God, but we chose to see ourselves separately from His energy. And that's when all hell broke loose, so to speak.

In chapter one of *The Grand Design* we read that the universe has no single history but every possible history and not even an independent existence. How could we have an independent existence if we depend on that great energy implanted in all of us before the world began? How could we have single history if we depend on those mysterious events, therefore histories, before the world began? Everyone's history is different. They are all reflections of our distant past, or better yet, of our initial condition.

The authors also mention that there are other paths to follow, which means there are other forms, such as universes, for us to understand what I've already written. There are many scripts we can follow. What we think we are choosing has already been scripted, for this reason the hypothesis of M-Theory and parallel universes was born.

I then, conclude that science needs religion. What scientists are doing is putting in their own words concepts they call principles or theories that are also mirrors of true self.

Ever since we humans have been on earth, we have feared the sun, gods, and God without realizing that the energy and power are in us. But while we keep insisting it is outside of us, we keep entertaining ourselves. Most of the time, we think we make original models with our brain. We think that what we see externally is real. Often, we repeat the same mistakes when making models; we may even create pain. Let's remember again that what we are doing is living over and over what has already happened. We cannot be separated from our origin.

Can what we think is external reality be thoroughly dissected for our advantage? I don't think so; nothing external exists, we already know that. Besides, what we are allowed to know is very limited and slowly showing up.

First of all, there is not much scientists can do with what they cannot see. In other words, they are allowed to go on in a very limited way. I already appear very quickly when we try to observe them, so they cannot be seen. In short, we cannot dissect what was created before the world began—call it energy, model-dependent realism, patterns, God, or whatever. We can only go as far as the big bang. But scientists admit there is more than that. As we go on dreaming, we can say that we do not need God, but we cannot say we do not need His energy.

Spontaneous Creation

One of my neighbors was always boasting about his exquisite apartment in Manhattan and the ladies he used to date. One day his doorbell rang. When he opened the door, he found himself face to face with a young woman holding a baby and smiling. It took him a while to remember their encounter and who she was.

Without saying a word to each other, she handed over the baby to him, and in as soft, gentle voice, said, "Here, take her, she is your daughter."

Astonished, he could hardly speak. Still, he managed to say, "How can this be? I hardly touched you."

"Yes, I know," she answered. "Her creation was spontaneous."

The making of a baby may be spontaneous, but like the universe, it is certainly not out of nothing.

Adults have 100 trillion cells in their bodies, but only one egg produces a baby together with one sperm. Then, they divide and become many. All the information there is, is contained in that winning cell, which is influenced by what we do and think. Some chemicals in the cells are very creative, others are not.

Creation and destruction exist everywhere, and it starts in our cells too, and so are the thoughts of war and peace. Everything has a beginning.

Young men produce 100 million sperm a day, and 500 million start to swim and compete to enter the ovum cell, but again only one can enter. The sperm has a hard time and encounters many obstacles on its journey.

Have you ever seen photographs of sperm moving in the womb? They seem to be swimming in an ocean. They look like bubbles, but with the shape of a head and tail. We owe these photos to Lennart Nilsson, a Swedish medical and scientific photographer.

As we have read in previous chapters, Hawking and Mlodinow

imagine that bubbles of boiling water make galaxies, stars, and us. Of course, the authors are referring to a different kind of bubble, but we never know what God plans to do next.

Words express patterns and models that were formed before we existed. As we know, life started in the sea before humans were created.

> Then God said, Let the waters abound with
> The abundance of living creatures, and let the firmament
> of the heavens. So, God created great sea creatures…
> And God blessed them, saying, "Be fruitful
> And multiply…"
>
> Genesis 1:20, 21, 22

Some of the details of creation before we existed are symbolized in what happened in the womb from conception up to the moment we were born. If we look at photos of the first instant of conception up to the moment we were born. If we look at photos of the first instant of conception to birth, we see what looks like a chaotic mass. Yet, Leonnart Nilson writes in A Child Is Born, in the chapter entitled "Fertilization," that there is order in chaos. Furthermore, we also find out that, "Instantaneously, numerous hereditary characteristics of the new individual are determined." This is a sign that we are predestined.

As we go on looking at more photos, we learn details not only about the historical formation of human beings, but we can also imagine the formation of the world around us.

In some photos, the embryo looks like a planet surrounded by light. Others look like a planet surrounded by light. Others look like the moon. Indeed, the formation of the blastocyst, which is followed by the embryo and then the fetus, has many stages, some of which may not be well-defined yet.

As described in *A Child Is Born,* every aspect of creation goes on according to time, which started at the big bang, so every step of creation was very well planned, organized, and structured in advance before time existed. Then it was manifested on earth, just like with our scripts. It all starts with the great journeys of the winning sperm and cell, until they fuse.

Cells have atoms, molecules, electrons, other substances, and DNA which provides codes for the information needed for our creation. They also include salvation and temptation. There is a void inside the atom, which may seem like an empty space, but there is pulsation and intelligence in there.

But the making of a baby would not happen if men and women did not have sex hormones. Photos of sex hormones are shown in crystalline form and look like diamonds. It should be no surprise to find out that diamonds are a woman's best friend, and also that we pick up models and patterns from billions of years ago before we were created. This concept reminds us of what has been written in this book. Is this a coincidence?

Our imagination seems to be beyond limits. It is also important to know that both male and female sex hormones are regulated by the brain with the proper thoughts such as, "Yes, I can accomplish whatever I want to accomplish."

We also have to be careful when buying clothes, decorating our environment, and even eating. As we see in the photos published in the above mentioned book, the color red shows a rise in temperature, even when we kiss, and that helps our creation. However, the color blue gives us a low temperature. It Is obvious, if we want excitement in our life, that we must think red and surround ourselves with red objects, clothes, and even eat red foods like radishes and lobsters. We must also kiss often.

As written in A Child Is Born, "we are strongly influenced by erotic stimulants called pheromones." These stimulants are secreted by both sexes, and their concentration rises during a kiss.

Whatever we do and whatever we think our thoughts are, we have to remember that God is watching our entertainment. He is the real Creator.

We are grateful to Leonnart Nilsson for showing us the first detailed pictures of human creation on earth. Like everything else on this planet, the information we are given is limited. Nilsson writes the fertilization, the moment the sperm and the egg fuse, remains a mystery. It happens in the Fallopian tube where "neither eye, nor camera had penetrated these recesses."

Furthermore, the cells behave in a mysterious way. At first, they seem the same and serve the same purpose, but later on "almost every cell is unlike every other." In the same page, Nilsson wonders, "How do the cells know what to become and which organ of the body to form?" They have codes and carry information as already mentioned. Who chooses? Who controls? Where could those codes come from? Certainly from a non-local reality, which we refer to in other chapters.

The first stage of the encounter between the sperm and the cell, known as blastocyst, which leads to fertilization, lasts about three weeks. Then it becomes an embryo, and it seems that some nerve cells are already formed.

In A Child Is Born, there are photos of some events of our creation that the author class that the author calls planets and lunar landing. There are colorful pictures of what happens to our cells. But there are halos around the cells. Those of us who have seen paintings and pictures of saints have observed the beautiful light around them, especially their heads. These are the halos, which in principle cannot be detected by the human eye.

Indeed, the miracle of life, is manifested everywhere. At the third week of conception, the embryo is less than an inch long; it looks like a tube with an opening on the top and another on the bottom. The organs must now be coordinated. The vertebral column looks like fish gills and Nilsson writes that the "embryo resembles a prehistoric animal." But the heart starts beating.

In week five, we see for the first time the embryo swimming in the fetal sac, and in the sixth week, it begins to look an extraterrestrial. By week seven, the embryo produces 100 thousand nerve cells per minute, and when the baby is born, there will be 100 billion. In the eight week, it goes from embryo to fetus and looks like "a space traveler in his capsule, complete with lifeline." When the fetus is about six months old, it is covered with hair all over.

When a baby is born, his body is wrinkled and looks old. Then he turns into a beautiful baby. This transformation may also happen when we die. I have a testimony from a witness who happens to be a distant family member. When her husband died, she was present as well as doctors and nurses. He had a serious health problem and had gone through a lot of pain and suffering. He was of advanced age. Within a few seconds after his death, and to the astonishment of everyone present, he changed from an old man to a teenager, exactly as she knew him when they met at school.

Does this mean that there is no death? According to modern physics, atoms do not die. Our cells have atoms. Do we need more proof that death is only physical and spirit is eternal?

In the Bible, we have a description of the event of the transfiguration of Jesus, known as the transfiguration on the mount, which was watched by some of his disciples.

> Now after six days Jesus took Peter James, and John his brother, led them up on a high mountain by themselves; and He was transfigured before them. His face shone like the sun, and His clothes became as white as the light... While he was still speaking, behold, a bright cloud overshadowed them: and suddenly a voice came out of the cloud, saying, This is My beloved Son, in whom I am very pleased. Her Him.
>
> Mathew 17:1, 2, 5

It is mentioned in A Child Is Born, in the chapter entitled "Labor and Delivery," that a baby goes through a lot of stress while being born, but the fetus is well prepared for the event. The great amount of the stress hormone secreted before birth is such that "it will never happen in later life." The great intelligence within us knows how to structure our lives in accordance with our needs.

At about ten to twelve weeks old, the fetus measures less than two inches; he jerks, moves and hiccups. By the thirteenth week, the eyes are developed but the eyelids remain closed until seven months old. Does this mean the fetus cannot see? This is an important question, because doctors have concluded that if they look inside the uterus "using a fetoscope with a light attached, the fetus tries to shield its eyes with its hands."

Dear reader, please rest and ponder.

Do you remember how often we say, "Some of us have eyes, but we are not able to see?" Now, we know that seeing is really beyond what eyes can see.

_____

_____

_____

Have you ever heard of events of transfiguration as described above? Have you witnessed them? What was your reaction?

_____

_____

_____

In the chapter titled "The Goldfish and Us," I described the story of a fish inside a curved bowl that could give the fish a distorted view of reality. As I read A Child Is Born, I noticed many photos of the fetus swimming in the fetal sac, which is like a balloon and therefore curved. I imagined this environment could give the fetus the first experiences of a distorted reality. Is it possible that God created us by putting us in a situation like the goldfish in the bowl so that we see a distorted view of reality? Even Hawking and Mlodinow have a similar question. Did God plan the fetal sac so that, while in the womb, we start to learn and see what is outside of us, and later in on life, we have to learn to value what is within us?

If the answers God would give these questions would be yes, then we could understand that our distorted view of reality while on earth is implanted in us when we are in the womb. What a wonderful discovery.

Over ten years ago, I wrote that I believed the whole universe is a womb. We are placed here to learn to discern between what is real and unreal, between what is true and what is false. Only by listening to our inner voice we can get clear answers. Our eyes are not even necessary; there is an ongoing communication within us that is beyond space and time. This is what happened to the fetus in the sac, described in this chapter. The fetus listened to the inner voice that warned it that the telescope light would distort its vision and not allow it to see the true invisible light that is always in communication with us; it all starts before we are in the womb. The fetus then covered its eyes with its hands. Who or what is communicating with the womb? I wonder how many times I've covered my eyes. How about you?

Have you ever heard about the prophet Jeremiah, as quoted below?

Then, the word of the Lord came to me saying: "Before I formed you in the womb I knew You; Before you were born I sanctified you; I ordained you a prophet to the nations."

Jeremiah 1:4-5

What else we learn while in the womb may seem a mystery. But in the end, it should not be because as soon as we are born, we start to show signs of what we have learned already. We must have been told about the whole script of our lives, and models and patterns must have been also implanted in us. Indeed, in nine months, we learn a lot. What an extraordinary energy created us!

I believe we even watch our own formation as we watch our own birth and death: we are prepared for everything in advanced. This may seem strange but it is trye. I gave the example of a person who changed from looking old to looking young right after his death. Now I'll give you a description of my own birth.

Years ago, I wrote to my mother and asked her to give me details of my birth. Her answer surprised and astonished me so much that I cried. Today, but only today, as I am writing this chapter, I understand what really happened and why. I thank God for His guidance.

Present at my birth were the midwife, one of my aunts, and a couple of my neighbors; one of them had been a male nurse during the World War I. I remember two major points that my mother mentioned. I was her only child. She was in her late twenties when I was born. My mother wrote that it was a beautiful birth. It lasted an unusual few hours. She added that I gave her an easy time- it seemed that I was always helping her during her ordeal. Furthermore, the moment I was born, I opened my eyes wide and looked at the whole room. Then, I closed my eyes and went to sleep. I never cried.

I guess, as I am writing this book, the time was right for me to find out what happens at birth and death. We exist in order to help each other.

In the end, everything I have written about for years comes from an education that originated before I was born. The script unfolds gradually. We are trained to realize that there is nothing new under the sun. This is a message to remind mankind that all scripts are written by someone who knew all about our needs before we were formed.

> All things are full of labor;
> Man cannot express it.
> The eye is not satisfied with seeing
> Nor the ear filled with hearing.
> That which has been is what will be,
> That which is done is what will be done,
> And there is nothing new under the sun.
> Is there anything of which it may be said.
> "See, this is new?"
> It has already been in ancient times before us.
> There is no remembrance of former things,
> Nor will there be any remembrance of things
> That are to come
> By those who will come after.
>
> Ecclesiastes 1:8, 11

Transformation

Our lives have many events that have been transformed for better or for worse. They all have the same aim- to help us accomplish our return.

For example, were you dismissed from your job which you planned to keep for a long time? How about going home the same day to tell your husband, and you found out he wants to divorce you?

The Bible is full of events that show us how much people's lives have been transformed and still continue to be.

In the Old Testament, we have the story of Ruth and her mother-in-law, Naomi. They were both widows and very poor. Yet, they chose to stay together even though Naomi insisted that Ruth should go somewhere else where there was more food than in the area they were living.

It was love that kept them together. In order to survive, Ruth had to pick up the grain left over in the field of a wealthy farmer named Boaz. This was done during the night. The grain was left there on purpose for poor people to pick it up and have something to eat. This event was called gleaning. Neither of the women were Jewish, yet Nami taught Ruth about God.

In the end, they were rewarded. God is always at work in this world. He gives choices of tasks that need to be accomplished in order to fulfill our mission. We may never know what it is. Eventually, Boaz married Ruth. They had a child named Obed, who became the father of Jesse. Then, Jesse became the father of David, the famous king of Israel. Consequently, Ruth was David's great-grandmother, which led to the lineage of the Messiah.

Rest and ponder.

Has your life ever gone from poverty to richness or, vice-versa? Did you ever wonder why?

_____

_____

_____

Have you noticed any other changes in your life, sometimes when you least expect? Did you like what happened?

_____

_____

_____

Do you ever wonder who does the transformation? What is the point of it?

_____

_____

_____

We have also an event in the Apostle Paul's life. In 2 Corinthians 12:7, Paul refers to "a thorn in the flesh" that was given to him. In spite of his great discomfort, he boasted that he was "taking pleasure in his infirmities" and concluded that "when I am weak, then I am strong."

Have you ever had a moment when you were sick and yet felt strong?

How about the Apostle John? He was exiled to the island of Patmos so that people could no longer listen to him. What happened to Apostle John while in exile? He started to write Revelation, the last chapter of the New Testament.

> Man proposes and God disposes.
>
> Thomas A. Kempis

Another example of transformation is the story of Joseph, a Jew, which starts in Genesis 37 and goes on until the end of Genesis. Joseph was loved by his father and hated by his brothers. When he was a teenager, his brothers sold him to merchants who in turn sold him to an Egyptian who had influence in Pharaoh's palace. After years of adventures in Egypt, Joseph became the governor. He was good at prophesying while others were so bad, they were ordered to be assassinated by the Pharaoh. The story of Joseph is an example of love, courage, forgiveness, political intuition, and reversal. It is also a great example of understanding our relationship with God, especially when Joseph tells his brothers that they "were not the ones that sent him to Egypt, God did that so that he could save many people alive" Genesis 45 And he saved not only Egyptians but also his family from starvation.

Have you ever felt great pains when your life turned around, and later on realized it was for your own good?

The Apostle Paul went from being a Jew to a Christian. He persecuted many Christians until one day he had a vision of Christ. Then, he converted and was persecuted to the point that he had to flee to Rome where he was born. He died there.

Relax and ponder.

Have you ever gone through events like this? Have you ever felt persecuted? Do you know of anyone that has been persecuted? Do you agree that it is to help us "return?"

_____

_____

_____

Science and Philosophy

In Greek, the word philo means love and sophy means wisdom. Philosophy, then, means love of wisdom. In accordance with a common proverb attributed to Cicero, 106 BC, philosophy is "knowledge of things human and divine, and of causes of which those things are controlled."

As per the above quote, the aim of philosophy is to help us live a better life by having and understanding "of things human and divine," which exist within all of us. But that cannot be achieved until we reach an understanding of our true cause. We need to experience the great energy within us; we need to practice. Who does not want to live a better life?

The authors of The Grand Design do not seem to agree with Cicero. In the first chapter, they mention that philosophy is dead because it "has not kept up with modern developments of science, particularly physics."

There are twentieth century writers and physicists who can be considered philosophers. I would like to mention some of them, which I've also quoted in You Can Remember Love (Bigote 2000).

Sir James Jeans in chapter five of The Mysterious Universe writes, "The universe begins to look more like a great thought than a great machine." The question is: who does the thinking? Only a higher power could have thought such thoughts. He also writes, "modern scientific theory compels us to think of the creator as working outside time and space, which are part of his creation, just as the artist is outside of his canvas." Here, the author is referring to the true observer, our Creator, who is unchanging and everlasting, the one that "hovers over the waters."

In chapter fifteen of the book titled The Universe and Dr. Einstein, Lincoln Barnett writes about physicist Niels Bohr, saying: "We are both spectators and actors in the great drama of existence." He is referring to us humans as observers in space and time, and also the fact that we are acting.

Physicist David Bohm writes in Wholeness and the Implicate

Order that "mind and body come from a dimension that is neither mind nor body." What could that dimension be? Certainly, only spirit. And, because of our misunderstandings, it was necessary for us to come to earth.

In Dialogues with Scientists and Sages, Bohm also refers to "an ocean of light,"28 which is or has the potential of everything. This ocean of light has energy and carries information about the entire universe. Where could that "ocean of light" be but everywhere, and therefore, inside us?

Nigel Calder, in Einstein's Universe, in the chapter entitled "Energy of Creation," mentions that "virtually all atoms in our bodies that are heavier than hydrogen were fashioned in the stars that expired before the sun and the earth come into being."29 In the above quote we have a reference to before the world began.

I consider Einstein the greatest philosopher of the twentieth century. His little formula $E=mc^2$, "sums up all action and creation of the universe. "30 This formula is philosophical. It has to do with the distribution of energy and the fact that the whole is in every part; that is, every piece of matter contains a great amount of energy. This means that even the smallest amount of anything on this planet, including in our bodies, has an extraordinary energy in it, and light is part of it. Matter, then, is frozen energy. This makes it easier for us to accept what happened just before the world was created and at creation.

When we were sent out of heaven, our energy froze. Then, a great intelligence interfered. That frozen energy was waiting to be activated and distributed, in the form of light, to form us and all things.

That great energy is in our DNA, which is in the atom and inside our cells; we receive it at conception. Remember what happened in the fetus when it covered its eyes because the false light was interfering with the true light.

A great quote attributed to Plato is, "The prison house is the world of sight."

The prison house is when we cannot see the unseen, such as

God who is in everything and in us. It is what prevents us from understanding what Jesus said, "I and My Father Are One" (John 10:30). We have to be careful and not misinterpret this Bible quote, which refers to being one in the form of spirit only.

St. Augustine wrote that we cannot be one as long as we are in the body form, that is, in the form of matter, as quoted in The Great Chain of Being (1936).

If all things were equal, all things would not be; for the multiplicity of kinds of things of which the universe is constituted--first, and second and so on, down to the creatures of the lowest grades--would not exist."

If all of us were equal, this world would not exist. It was designed to represent differences and, there-fore, separation. It was designed to hide spirit, our true self. It is our task to undo separation.

Calder also mentions that Einstein's equation "provides a modern version of Genesis and Revelation."

Dear reader, please rest and ponder. You may consider that the light of the world is not pure light because it has mass. If we meditate on thinking of light, we have to ask for His help.

What have you found out about yourself? Aren't you a philosopher?

Stephen Hawking's A Brief History of Time was published in 1988. He writes, "This whole vast construction exists only for our sake." He is implying that it is necessary for us to be here, which is the same thought that philosopher Plato, who lived about 500 BC, had. In his conclusion, Hawking writes that if we ever find a complete theory of everything, "it will be the ultimate triumph of human reason for then we would know the mind of God." In the same book, he asks, "Can there really be such a unified theory? Or are we perhaps just chasing a mirage?" As I read A Brief History of Time, I concluded that Hawking, like Einstein and other scientists, are philosophers.

However, the greatest surprise came with the publication in 2010 of The Grand Design. As previously mentioned, Hawking and Mlodinow write on the last page about the future M-Theory, which will hopefully be the complete theory of everything. They mention that once discovered, it will answer all our questions and "it is not necessary to invoke God."

This conclusion made me sad. Is it possible that Dr. Hawking is no longer a philosopher?

He has been blessed with a great mind, and I still believe that in the end, everyone is a philosopher and that includes Stephen Hawking.

The Sheep and
The Shepherd

My father was never a big talker. However, his favorite sentence to me while I was growing up was, "It's all in the mind. It's all in the mind. It's all connected." Whenever he mentioned these sentences, he used to point his index finger at his forehead. He never went any further. He never gave me details of what goes on in the mind or what the mind is about.

So, I left home at age twenty-one, five months, and one hour. I was born in March, left in August, exactly five months after my twenty-first birthday. The reason I know it was one hour is because the train from Lisbon to Paris and London left at one in the afternoon, and I was born at noon.

I never regretted that day. I started planning to go to England before I was fourteen years old. I told my parents that I wanted to go and study in London. They always answered, "Yes, yes, of course." But they never offered to help me. I never told them that I want to find out about the mind.

Then, I began to tell myself to be reasonable, and wait until I was more mature. In the mean-time, I worked as a correspondent, writing letters in English for a small firm that imported fabrics. I saved all the money I could and waited until that day in August-a day that I will remember with joy, love, and gratitude.

When I arrived in London, even the grass jumped with joy. Happiness was everywhere-inside me and all around. It seemed that my eyes had changed. I was seeing the world with different eyes.

Freedom. Freedom. I kept repeating to myself. I was also thinking about what I had left behind, besides my family. I had left a strict dictatorial government. Like Albert Einstein, I deplore anyone that restricts freedom. We need to be free to choose, even to make mistakes.

I had never seen parks like I saw in London, nor people relaxing on the grass. I don't think that was ever allowed at that time in Portugal. I lived in London for about four years, with occasional visits to Lisbon. Then, I lived in Switzerland, France, and one day, I arrived in the US, where I have been for four decades.

My mother passed away before my father. He spent the last four years of his life in a nursing home. It was always a pleasure to visit him. We used to spend hours playing dominos and saying a few words to each other. Neither he nor I would ever get tired, and we realized we had to separate only when it was time for his dinner.

The nursing home was located in a small town near Lisbon. It was surrounded by pine trees and shrubs. There was a garden and some land separating the two buildings, one for men and one for women and couples.

Walking up the hill to catch the bus just before sunset was always a delightful experience. I knew I was going to watch something so unique and so thrilling that would keep me in awe for some time. Like everything in life, sometimes we have a tendency to forget even the most challenging events, but I never forgot this one.

On the top of the hill from my father's nursing home was a huge open space. Next to it was a farm, where about one hundred sheep used to bask in the sunshine after a day of pasturing. I used to sit under a pine tree and watch them. The sheep had to go by my father's nursing home every time they went in and out of the farm. Sometimes, when they went by, I used to follow them up the hill to catch the bus. They always proceeded calmly and in unison until they arrived at the farm. I watched them go in; they never bumped into each other.

On day, everything changed. I noticed some sheep were moving around the farm, especially the smaller ones. The sounds were tremendous but very pleasant. It was almost like an orchestra rehearsing for the next show. At first it was just "Baa. Baa. Baa," Then, it sounded differently "Baaaaa, Baaaa."

I had to satisfy my curiosity. One day, I approached the shepherd.

"Sir, Sir." I had to yell and wave my hand at him. He was on the other side of the field. He finally approached me. I told him that everybody in the nursing home knew him and his sheep, and I heard men commenting on his lifestyle, apparently envying him and calling him "the rich shepherd." They wondered why, since the sheep were worth a lot of money, he did not sell his flock and retire.

He was shocked. He told me right away that he would never do that. "I have always been happy with my sheep."

I am the good shepherd. The good shepherd gives His life for the sheep. But the hireling, he who is not the shepherd, who does not owned the sheep, sees the wolf coming, and leaves the sheep and flees, and the wolf catches the sheep and scatters them. The hireling flees because he is a hireling and does not care about the sheep.

John 10:11

In this quote, Jesus is favoring ownership. When we own something, we take good care of it. We also give our lives for our sheep.

Then, I asked the shepherd what was going on; why had the sheep changed the tone of their "Baa. Baa"?

"Miss, there are three types of sheep. The male is called the ram, the female is the ewe, and the smaller ones are the lambs. What you hear at this time of the day are the mothers calling their little ones to be fed."

"How can this be?" I said surprised. "There are so many of them. They all look alike. How can they find each other? Just by the sounds of their mothers' baas?"

"They know, Miss, they know." And he looked up and pointed to the sky. "It is all connected," he added. Then, he told me that if I wanted to know more about the sheep, I could come earlier and join them in the valley. Unfortunately, I could not accept his offer because I had to go and attend to my father.

I never forgot this shepherd. He did not sell his happiness. He helped me realize that I had never sold my happiness either, even though I could have chosen to go back home, especially when I had to endure some difficulties, while living abroad.

This good shepherd reminded me of my father's saying, "It's all in mind. It is all in the mind. It is all connected." I finally understood the answer after years of travelling. I had returned home.

Rest and Ponder.

Have you ever wondered what kind of communication there is among people and animals that does not need words? Has this type of experience ever happened to you?

_____

_____

_____

Do you think the mind plays a major role in our lives?

_____

_____

_____

The latest book of the well-known physicist, Fred Alan Wolf, is entitled Time Loops and Space Twists. How God Created the Universe. He writes, "Mind may not arise from the brain, but actually exists in the whole universe-the Mind of God, so to speak, as a tachyonic mind field."3% For this physicist, our brain is like a radio receiver. We receive information from a great mind. Tachyonic mind field is part of the string theory, which may help the development of the unified theory.

There is a message in everyone and in every event we are faced with. Something in the mind of the little lambs was connected to their mothers'.

It is unfortunate that most of us are used to thinking that we humans many times behave like lambs, weak and submissive. We forget what spirit and sometimes even science teach us that there is an intelligence that is beyond intelligence, an energy that connects all there is, and that includes animals, birds, and all other living creatures like us. There is no need for words. We are all mirrors to each other.

Everything That Happens Has a Cause

It has always been mankind's wish to dissect and analyze God, which is the same as saying we want to find out what happened before the world began. Curiosity is part of the human condition.

There are problems with the word wish. One of them has to do with time, which, as we have read, started at the big bang. The fact that we cannot analyze what happened then causes frustration in scientists, philosophers, believers, and non-believers in God, men, women-in short, in all of us. Our wish cannot be accomplished.

Emmanuel Kant, the eighteenth century philosopher, arrived at the same conclusion in his Critic of Pure Reason. He realizes that the problem of philosophy has to do with God, freedom of will, and immortality. He explains that metaphysics is the science that seeks a solution to these problems but, of course, it is structured in such a way that it does not allow us to investigate.

Herein lies the mystery of life, a concept that is very difficult for most people to accept. We can always reason, but reason has its limits. Intuition plays a major role in our experiences. Not all of us can become supermen and superwomen.

Other words also play a major role in our reasoning. One of the words that I've already quoted and I find most intriguing is a priori. In accordance with Webster's Third New International Dictionary (1961), a priori means made before and "without examination, or analysis, independent of experience, intuitively."3" Our experiences while here on earth have no effect on the events that happened before the earth began. For some time, I believed the understanding of a priori ended with the above-mentioned dictionary description. However, the more

I read, the more information I find that adds to the topic of this book the information helps to clarify and understand its concepts.

For Kant, there are two aspects of a priori. For instance, the title of this chapter, "Everything That Happens Has a Cause," expresses a universality and a necessity which experience cannot explain. In other words, our true cause, also known as the first cause, cannot be examined. This example is what Kant calls "a pure a priori statement."

Furthermore, the word necessity reminds me of what I learned from Plato and the Bible-it was necessary for us to come to earth in order to learn to return.

Then Kant gives us what he calls "an impure a priori statement"-"Every change has a cause. " It is impure because change comes from our experience on earth, but our true cause does not; it is changeless, therefore it can only come from Spirit, and that is the reason why we cannot separate our-selves from it.

Kant asks, more or less, the same question as Hawking and Mlodinow is there a knowledge independent of experiences and even of all sensuous impressions?

The answer to this question is yes. But, we must keep in mind that the word knowledge in this sense can refer only to our true cause. Therefore, we have to consider what might have happened before the world began, which will show that we have knowledge independent of our experiences on earth. The knowledge that we acquire while on this planet comes mainly from our schooling and our home; it is, therefore, illusory compared with the real knowledge from spirit.

Again, let's go back to what is mentioned in the chapter entitled "Spontaneous Creation." There, we read about the ten-to-twelve-week-old fetus, measuring less than two inches. Its eyes were closed, yet it covered them with its hands when a light from the fetoscope shone on them. The fetus was not completely physically formed and had not lived on earth, yet it protected itself from the effects of the fake light. It must have known already all about the true light which is everywhere, as we have read.

We can then say that while we are in the womb, we are receiving a priori knowledge, although we have not yet experienced life on earth. We are, how-ever, experiencing some event that changes the environment inside the womb, like artificial light.

Cause comes from before the world began. Change is based on our experiences, while in full body form or not. It is interesting to learn that God allows our changes. He gives us choices so that we learn that He is the eye behind all events, and our true cause never left us.

Dear reader, please rest and ponder.

Can you imagine the influence of our true cause in your life? Do you understand that it is changeless?

_____

_____

_____

Can you see the difference between what is true and what is false? Does the fact that truth is changeless, surprise you?

_____

_____

_____

Were you aware of what was happening within you? Were you grateful for the experience?

_____

_____

_____

_____

The impure a priori statements manifest our duality; we are here but we are also up there. Jesus, too, was both human and divine.

Metaphysics is in accordance with Albert Einstein's little formula $E=mc^2$, which was previously mentioned. One cell carries all the information there is. We cannot separate ourselves from our true cause, even while we are being formed in the womb.

Some philosophers have stated that metaphysics is an illusion. This was just their wish. Kant claimed that the problem with his affirmation was that the sciences, such as math and physics, are also a priori but impure. In other words, the real cause that is, the origin of sciences like math and physics-came from before the world began; therefore, it is pure, and its origins cannot be experienced or dissected here on earth. But once we start experimenting with sciences, we affect changes and they become impure, consequently sciences are also illusions.

Such experiments are like a virgin; she was born pure but loses her purity after her first sexual encounter. All we are doing is working with information that is filtered, so to speak, from a real and original source to keep us entertained, thinking that by ourselves we can discover unity in everything. No wonder even the sciences become impure. In other words, all of us are illusions working with illusions. We wish this was not true.

The fact that we experience $1+1=2$ cannot deny the fact that $1+1=1$, as in the statement from Jesus, "I and My Father Are One" (John 10:30). This is pure a priori. Cause and effect cannot be separate. That must be the reason why the word cause causes so many difficulties among all of us, especially scientists and philosophers. No one on earth can dissect what in written in Jesus's affirmation. It cannot be experienced either.

Life is simple, that is, if we want to accept the facts. It may take time, but as it is written in the Bible:

Everything Has Its Time

To everything there is a season,
A time for every purpose under heaven:
A time to be born,
And a time to die,
A time to plant,
And a time to pluck what is planted;
A time to kill,
And a time to heal;
A time to break down,
And a time to build up;
A time to weep,
And a time to laugh;
A time to mourn,
And a time to dance;
A time to cast away stones,
And a time to gather stones;
A time to embrace,
And a time to refrain from embracing;
A time to gain,
And a time to lose;
A time to keep,
And a time to throw away;
A time to tear,
And a time to sew;
A time to keep silence,
And a time to speak;
A time to love,
And a time to hate;
A time of war,
And a time of peace.

Ecclesiastes 3:1-8

The Grand Manipulator and His Buttons

Do you realize you have a Grand Manipulator within you? It was implanted in your cells and starts to activate in a shrewd way when we are in the womb, as described in the chapter, "Spontaneous Creation."

If you are confused or resistant to these ideas do not be surprised, many of us feel the same way. As we have read, our preconceived ideas can cause great damage but we are learning to face them with courage and handle them.

The mission of the Grand Manipulator is to see if he can torment us with his temptations. He knows what he is doing. We must learn from him and not let ourselves be tempted.

How does he accomplish his mission? He pushes buttons in our mind. But first he has to know what our needs are then he uses them as bait. He knew Jesus had fasted for forty days and forty nights. He assumed Jesus was hungry and would fall for his temptations, as we read in the following quote from Matthew 4:3, which I've also quoted in the chapter "Can We Change Our Models."

If you are the Son of God, command that these stones become bread.

Jesus could easily consent to his request, but that meant the grand manipulator would succeed in making Jesus press the buttons he chose. In this quote we can see how shrewd the manipulator thinks he is, and he uses buttons. Of course, Jesus did not follow his instructions, Jesus knew he had within Himself another button that He pressed-the Spirit's. Consequently, He answered according to the Scriptures.

Why does the grand manipulator find it so easy to accomplish his mission most of the time? Let's not forget that ours is a dreaming universe, therefore, we are also hallucinating, as some scientists say. Under these circumstances, we can easily be hypnotized and manipulated.

Here is a simple example: If you are a single woman with three kids and a man comes to you and says he loves you so much that he wants to marry you and help raise your kids, you certainly have a lot of thinking to do. You must decide to accept or refuse his offer. You can choose which button to press, but before you do, watch how he handles his friends, his co-workers, and his family, because, sooner or later, he will treat you the same way. This situation can be applied to any of us. I am not saying that men and women are bad or good.

Please rest and ponder

Do you or anyone you know ever encountered a situation as described above? Or even another situation?

What was the reaction?

_____

_____

_____

What have you learned from this example?

_____

_____

_____

We may also ask, where does the grand manipulator's energy come from? It can come only from the same source as ours, since there is only one atom. The reader may also wonder how can this energetic manipulator be allowed to interfere with our energy? First of all, he is only allowed if we let him. Apart from that, this is how the universe was set up, and no one can change that. The Bible teaches that Spirit led Jesus to be tempted, so that he could show us a way out!

We may not have read the Bible, but we all know the story of Adam and Eve, where we have one of the greatest examples of the job assigned to the grand manipulator which is to convince mankind with his creepy ways to press his buttons. And they were easily convinced, and so do most of us.

Energy has a unified center that attracts and pulls us inward towards itself to unity and peace. The big circles around the center disperses our energy and splits us.

The Grand Manipulator has a mission, Jesus has a mission, and so do all of us.

Our mission is to realize that, like Jesus, we have choices, and it all depends which button we choose to press. Jesus mission was also to help us see the "unseen." Now, it is up to us to choose again and again.

War, Peace and the M-Theory

We know from life experiences, from reading the history of the world and the Bible that wars are always happening. If there are fifty years of peace, it means mankind is preparing to attack because during those fifty years, the war within each individual doesn't end.

War is therefore constant. It is always going on within us and around us. It is the major form we have chosen in order to be entertained while we are on earth. It is painful. But we must like it; otherwise, we would not make it ongoing.

War is conflict within us that is projected out-ward. What we see happening all around us is a reflection of what goes on inside us. It is a constant cycle. War is interference in the flow of the light from our friends, family, enemies, countries, and above all, ourselves.

So, where is the solution? It can only be within us where the cause came from.

Buddha was right when he wrote:

> You may conquer in a battle a thousand times,
> A thousand men,
> Yet he is the best of conquerors
> Who conquers himself.
> We are all a reflection of each other; what I think, you think too.
> I celebrate myself and sing myself. And what I assume you shall
> assume, For every atom belonging to me as good belongs to you.
> -Walt Whitman, "Song of Myself"

We have read that we came from one cell which contains all the information, all the intelligence there is, and all the energy necessary for us to exist. We have imagined that the one cell split into many. We created a dreaming universe, so say some scientists, and that is where the war is-in the dream of the split. This is how conflict is shared-with the split, not with the one.

We share conflict with the split because we believe John, Joe, Mary, or whoever is parading in our mind has hurt us in the past. This causes a painful illusion. In order to solve this problem, we have to reach that energy and intelligence in us. We have to believe that we have free will to choose.

If we read Genesis, and meditate on it, we'll see that some sort of a conflict, a rebellion, happened before the world began, and, therefore, in heaven. As I have already mentioned, the details of this event are not for us to know at least, not while we are on this planet. The solution to this rebellion happened right away; Jesus manifested this accomplishment in his sentence, "I and My Father are One" (John 10:30). He is letting us know that there was unison before space and time were created at the big bang.

In chapter two, I mention the serpent, good and bad angels, and other characters that showed up, and nowhere does it say they were created on earth like Adam and Eve. So they had to exist in heaven, and there they rebelled. A split happened before the world began. All was programmed so that although the rebellion started in heaven, it had to be trans-posed to the earth, as a test to see if we could correct evil. Although we hope one day to have peace, it is apparent that it is not here, on this planet, that we'll solve our conflicts.

In order to save us, our Maker has to interfere again, as He did when he created the earth. The creation of the earth was not fiction; that great intelligence was not dreaming. What is fiction is the form of the dream that we have chosen as we follow the different paths here on earth and keep looking out-ward for our solutions.

So, let's get ready to face the continuation of our dream, which too often looks like a terrible night-mare. It seems we are willing to let it go on until we have enough, and let God save us again, or until He decides to take action.

Scientists, too, are contributing to our ongoing dream by thinking that by themselves they can dis-cover the theory of everything. As previously mentioned, they named it M-Theory.

It is mentioned in the second chapter that M-Theory predicts many universes. How did physicists and mathematicians arrive at the concept of M-Theory and also many universes, known as parallel universes?

Before we proceed, we must take into account that in spite of the fact that we are living in a dreaming universe, we can and must learn from our dreams. Parallel universes will show us that we have many choices, including looking at twins of ours living in other universes. We must not be afraid of discovering the possibility of something new about ourselves that hopefully will help us handle our emotions. We must get used to our own science fiction movies. We must have an open mind. Why should you be scared while reading this book, if I was not scared while researching and writing it for months? Let's pause for a moment.

Let your thoughts go on in your mind, then stop and write them down.

_____

_____

_____

How many did you write?

Do you realize that each thought opened up another dimension, that is, another universe? To put it in simple terms; each thought gave you another chance. Each thought represented a universe with a twin of yours or someone else's. For example, maybe you thought of becoming a writer. Well, there is a universe where you are a successful writer, or maybe you like Napoleon so much that you wished he was still alive there is a universe where he is still alive!

We read that scientists have concluded that according to the uncertainty principle, we are dealing with illusions, ours is a dreaming universe, and so are we. All of us believe in what does not correspond to reality. The Bible conveys the same message, as already quoted:

Wake up from your sleep.

Roman 13:11

Because physicists are dealing with what they can-not see, they use mathematics to arrive at their theories. However, as we have read, mathematics

becomes impure as soon as it is used by humans. Scientists then, deal with hypothesis, as in the case of M-Theory.

It should be interesting to know that Professor Hawking, in A Brief History of Time, chapter one, writes that "a theory is just a model and exists in our mind only." Theories proved today may be dis-proved tomorrow.

In the meantime, some physicists claim that "M" stands for membrane, while others prefer to define "M" as magic or mystery.

What led to the hypothetic M-Theory? Apparently it started with Albert Einstein, who found out that besides height, width, and length, there is also another dimension, which he called "time." Although he imagined there are still more than four dimensions, he died without completing his research.

Years later and while scientists thought that matter was made out of particles, which of course, no one can see, they found out that inside the particles there are strings. That led to the string theory and the possibility of many more dimensions and therefore, many universes. Scientists concluded there is music in the universe. We are musical. There are vibrations everywhere, including in us, that contain information and energy.

The string theory also led to the conclusion that everything in the universe is connected to one structure. They envision this structure to be like a mem-brane, which is like a tissue that connects parts of our bodies. Therefore, string theory, the possibility of many universes, and M-Theory were born.

Can M-theory in the end help mankind? Only if it leads us to embrace the "unseen," that oneness, that great energy in all of us.

Reading about modern physics and especially M-Theory is a wonderful challenge. Trying to understand it is very hard, since it has to do with quantum physics, also known as new physics, which physicists say no one understands.

But we say the same about God. Some of us say He is hard to understand, others say that no one understands Him. Perhaps if we can see love in the M-theory, we can begin to understand. Science, especially new physics, helps us see the oneness between God and us. No one has ever seen God, and no one has ever seen an atom, electron, etc., as already mentioned, yet they exist everywhere, and therefore within us in the form of energy. All of us have one thing in common; "the unseen", which is another name for oneness.

In the end, there are events, things, and people in our lives that we do not understand, but we must have faith and learn from them.

Is it hard to understand God because we can't see Him? Imagine how hard it must be for some scientists to work all their lives with what they cannot see. Indeed, what is unseen, such as the electron is what scientists claim provides us with the necessary energy for our existence here on earth.

Although electrons exist inside the atoms, and in us, new physics teaches that they leave the atom, split into many pieces, and emit radiation, which is electricity; therefore, we can say we are electric. Furthermore, they claim the electron exists simultaneously and everywhere. We can conclude that the same happens to all of us. Indeed, our dreams expand into the infinite.

Besides energy, the electrons have information and intelligence. This is how we are able to explore and extend our thoughts, wishes, and dreams. For instance, someone who does not like his or her mother-in-law may wish she never existed. According to new physics there is a universe where she never existed, and there is another universe where she is the sweetest mother-in-law anyone can imagine. In that universe, she lives in perfect harmony with all members of her family. This is what some scientists call parallel universes, multiple universes, alternative universes, and even ghostly universes. Other scientists, such as the authors of Grand Design, in chapter 6, p.136, 142-4 refer to other universes, of multiverse concept, and mention that universes with life like ours are rare, and "that some people make a great mystery of this idea..." But the concept of many universes, they say, is part of modern physics.

I believe that any thoughts we have constitute a universe, and it is all within us. Imagine the power of our mind. Some of the universes are copies of ours; we can't see them, but they can see us, and even communicate with us. I hope the reader now under-stands what non-local communication really is. Here are some real examples: a mother is mourning the death of her son. The son is right there, and he says, "Mother, I am here!" She can neither see, nor hear him. Another mother died, she tells her daughter, "We are closer than you think!" The daughter hears, but she cannot see. A man died, he tells his best friend, "I see you all the time. America is so beautiful!" She heard him.

A single and lonely French woman living in New York dreams that she has a lovely husband. He watches her and assures her of his love for her. She wakes up, and for a few seconds hears him speaking French. He caresses her while saying she is never alone.

We don't need science to confirm our experiences; the confirmation is handled between us and the unseen. If this woman could keep remembering the experience and use an affirmation such as, "I'm always being caressed," she could be healed of her loneliness. She needs to have faith and switch the buttons she is pushing, without denying her original condition.

All our thoughts-past, present, and future-have been scripted and may be recorded in parallel universes since before the world began. For example, if while talking to someone you say that you are getting married to John Joe, rest assured that you are putting in your own words what is written in another universe. However, there is a different universe where you are divorcing John Joe. And a friend of yours somehow tapped into that universe and told you that you will divorce him. Of course, you got mad at her and asked her where did she get that idea from, but she did not know the answer, or she may even admit that "something" told her that.

We are receiving non-local messages from parallel universes, or multiple universes, or other universes or whatever we want to call them, twenty-four hours a day. Unfortunately, we are not educated to recognize and even appreciate what is happening around us.

A very popular example among scientists is that Elvis Presley is still alive.

In accordance with parallel universes, there is one universe where he is alive, and another universe where he never existed. The unfolding of wars could have been entirely different; there is a universe where Second World War never happened. Imagine, if many people had concentrated on that universe, our history would be entirely different, for better or for worse.

As we can see, according to modern physics, ours is a ghostly universe indeed.

Enter by the narrow gate; for wide is the gate and broad is the way that leads to destruction, and there are many who go in by it. Because narrow is the gate and difficult is the way which leads to life, and there are few who find it.

Matthew 7:13

This quote from Matthew reveals that parallel universes represent our many choices: "for wide is the gate and broad is the way that leads to destruction..."

The other gate is difficult, so we choose the easy way out, and this is what we do when our hallucinations lead us to the extremes, and back to our illusory world of uncertainties.

Then, in the next quote, we are advised to follow the example of the ant who is certain of what she is doing.

Go to the ant, you sluggard!

Consider her ways and be wise, Which, having no captain, Overseer or ruler, Provides her supplies in the summer, And gathers her food in the harvest.

Proverbs 6:6-8

The Brazilian movie of 1976 titled Dona Flor and Her Two Husbands depicts in a simple and funny way parallel universes without any reference to science.

We can then conclude that in accordance with modern physics, parallel universes are worlds that exist next to ours. We don't need to travel to visit them, we can imagine communicating with them as they do with us!

Rest and ponder on this: All creatures, all things, and all people are together in our mind and beyond.

_____

_____

_____

Have you experienced events as described in this chapter? Were you afraid? What did you learn from them?

_____

_____

_____

Which gate do you usually follow? Why? What are your thoughts about the gate you have chosen?

_____

_____

_____

We have read that scientists hope M-Theory will help us unify everything. That means that all universes, all beings, and all things have to be part of a single whole, including parallel universes. We could not exist if that unity did not vibrate within us.

As we have read, some of them have life like ours. They are our twins, and there is an infinite number of them, as there is an infinite number of our thoughts, dreams, and wishes. They are connected to us, and we depend on them our electrons exist here and there.

Physicist Fred A. Wolf, in Parallel Universes, refers to Hawking believing that the universe always follows laws of physics, even before big bang, and there was no observer and no uncertainty then (Wolf 1988). This is a great confirmation of what is written in the Bible: only what is true and eternal is real, and can never be observed, that is, dissected by us, humans. Why? Because as we have read what we observe, we change, and we cannot change what is changeless and was created with certainty. We saw that in the example I gave of the chair: our light mingled with the light from it, and we have an effect on what we observe.

We should rejoice because modern physics is opening our minds to the fact that there is no uncertainty in heaven.

That great energy and intelligence some of us call God has an unlimited power to create all there is including Himself, therefore He creates everything that happened, before, now, and after. He does not need to observe what He created. He is certain of what He made. He is the observer only of our uncertainties which came from the chaos that we caused in our mind when we started to rebel and started to dream of a split. He is watching us and will interfere whenever is needed, especially when we ask for His help. He is the unchanging observer.

The Bible describes many events that we may call miracles. However, as I already mentioned, miracles are nothing but our return to our original condition of being One, as we read in the following quote, when Joshua needed daylight to fight a battle and asked for the Lord's help.

"Sun, stand still over Gibeon; And Moon, in the Valley of Aijalon. So the sun stood still, and the moon stopped, till the people had

revenge upon their enemies...So the sun stood still in the midst
of heaven, and did not hasten to go down for about a whole day.

Joshua 10:12-13 NKJV

Recently, some NASA scientists working together with astronauts
have researched and concluded that the missing day story described
in Joshua's above quote is true. Of course, many people from all walks
of life avoid to reveal this great event in modern science. NASA, of
course, has tried to prove with their uncertainties that the story is
not true. They will continue to be entertained by denying themselves
and others the truth.

We are not the only culture working on this event. Other cultures,
far more ancient than ours, have also contributed to such revelation
and are systematically ignored.

Let's recall that atoms, electrons, and so forth also existed before
the earth was formed. And the non-local communication is on-going.
Wolf concludes that parallel universes existed before time and before
we were created. These ideas are very important for the theme of this
book; they also confirm what I have written about the script in my
previous publications, and my belief that all events have been scripted
before the world began. Professor Wolf has imagined that a record
of all events must exist somewhere: parallel universes could be the
answer. Remember the rebellion, the serpent, Jesus, and so forth? They
were all choices and therefore events scripted before the creation of
the earth. What follows is a quote referring to Christ.

He indeed was foreordained before the foundation of the
world, but was manifested in these last days for you who
through Him believe in God, who raised Him from the dead
and gave Him glory, so that your faith and hope are in God.

Peter 1:18-20.

Dear reader: Please rest and ponder on this quote.
Can you see the confirmation of the message that I am trying to

convey in this book that all events happened before the foundation of the world; then they were manifested on earth?

Events that happened in the past and future may happen right now. We have the example of archeological research, which may bring us news of our past that will influence our future. Also, in spite of all our scientific advances, we have yet to find out how ancient Egyptians mummified their mummies. Our present, then, depends on the past and future.

As we have read, physicists found out that there is one structure which they called a membrane that envelops everything. As they researched further and further, they found out that there are more mem branes and more universes which led to the possibility that there were more than one bang. And, this means that there is a possibility of more than one big bang. Others wonder if there was a big bang at all.

We are indeed surrounded by uncertainties.

Think well folks: to keep us entertained, that great intelligence and energy within us created an infinite number of universes, to show us our choices which have already been scripted and chosen. This led to the M-Theory. This is where mankind is now, but sometime in the future, we'll be told about other theories, opening up what we believe to be new roads to learning. And a hardworking individual, in this case, a physicist or a mathematician, will win prizes for discovering what has already been written and accomplished before the world began.

Thanks to the great intelligence within us, we can actually grasp what a parallel universe is showing us. But in our hallucinations, sometimes we are not aware of what we are doing or what is happening to us.

It is ironic they hope the hypothetical M-Theory once discovered will show there is no need for God, while at the same time, His mysterious and incomprehensive energy manifests everywhere in a way that lead us on the road to Him.

It is also ironic that while for some scientists there is no God, and for others there is no need for God, scientists working with the large Hadron Collider, built underground between France and Switzerland, informed the world that by the year 2012 they hope to locate God Particle. Is this a play on words?

We know that it is all in the mind leading us to the beyond.

The authors of The Grand Design hope the M-theory will be a model that proves "the universe creates itself, and therefore there is no need for God," Such theory must "predict finite results for quantities that can be measured" and must be "confirmed by observation."*"

Part of the description of M-Theory, "the universe creates itself," may be inspired by what has been written that "God creates Himself."

I think scientists are dismissing the fact that there is an observer, known as the unchanging observer. He has a constant eye on our form of entertainment, including the M-Theory. Do scientists intend to put the unchanging observer out of business?

No one can measure love, truth, and eternity, they are real; everything else does not exist, or better yet, it seems to exist only while we are in the illusion of space and time.

Furthermore, as we have read, some scientists arrived at the conclusion that there was no observer before big bang, and no uncertainty: these are very important observations. Why should God be observing Himself? Should He not be certain of what He is doing?

How about the uncertainty principle? How can they predict finite results? As already mentioned, according to this principle, we produce only approximations or probabilities-we are limited by our observations.

It is true, nothing is impossible. But to achieve the impossible requires an extraordinary energy and intelligence which is beyond our comprehension. Since the beginning of time, we have been trying to comprehend that intelligence, but to no avail.

We know miracles can happen; however, in order to perform miracles we need to armor ourselves with true love, so that the energy in us can move even mountains. Each of us are given gifts which benefit all, as mentioned in 1 Corinthians 12:8-10.

For to one is given word of wisdom through the Spirit, to another the word of knowledge through the same Spirit, to another faith by the same Spirit, to another gifts of healing by the same Spirit, to another the working of miracles, to another prophecy..."

In the meantime, the show goes on. They expect the M-Theory will hopefully unify everything, including all the universes. Since we are part of the uni-verse, we must also be included. All will be unified, a planet of peace at last, so they imagine the dream of all dreams. This reminds me of the Tower of Babel which was destroyed because God was not involved in its construction.

Do we have to wait for this theory to unify us, which may never happen? Please, don't wait. Let's end the war within us now! We know that unity exists inside us. Let's work on accepting those models now. We are all scientists: our brain is a scientific laboratory. We are learning that science confirms our faith, and faith equals Love.

The Fruit-Stand Vendor

I have already mentioned how important it is to take care of ourselves our bodies, our thoughts. Now I'd like to write about what I've learned from my illness.

All my life I suffered from female problems; 1 have also had cancer and TB. I remember during one of my major operations, I had intravenous therapy for so long that both of my hands were in bad shape. When the therapy ended I cried not because of pain but because I was thanking God for the experiences. From that time on, I promised to use my hands for healing. I had no idea why I was speaking like that, but after some time I started to write my first book.

One day, I was walking on Broadway on my way to the hospital for treatment. I was aware of a message from my inner self directing me to a corner towards a fruit stand. Although I felt peaceful, my heart felt as if it was coming out of my body. As I approached the fruit stand, I noticed a very young vendor standing right there staring at me and smiling. It was as if he was waiting for me. To my great surprise, as I approached him, I watched in awe how rays of light were pouring onto him, starting from right above his head all the way down. The rays of light dissipated just before they reached his legs. The event lasted only an instant. It was faster than the lightning from a thunderstorm.

Now I can say that I know how fast the faster-than-light goes. I've seen it. Now I know the importance of an instant. Although I cannot observe the origin of the event, I can certainly guess. I too was smiling and wondering if he saw flashes of light pouring on me. I know that our light mingles with the light of whatever we are observing. For a few seconds, we stared at each other, in awe. I had never seen him before. He was almost too beautiful and calm to be true. I bought fruit and did not comment on the event, although I saw him often after our first encounter.

The encounter with the fruit-stand vendor was programmed

non-locally, before the world began in a realm that we cannot understand. Those of us who go through such experiences recognize, like I did, how much there is to learn from everyone we encounter while here on earth. We are all connected by an energy that unites everything and everyone there is on this planet. The light/energy in me is the same as in you but it is invisible.

As already mentioned, non-local communication is everywhere; it is usually invisible, and very rarely it is visible. Most of the time we do not recognize that there is an on-going communication beyond space and time. It is part of us. It is implemented in our cells. It is the intelligence that keeps us as one. And only that intelligence really knows what else was happening between the young fruit-stand vendor and myself. Why was it programmed this way? Was it just a coincidence?

Usually, coincidences refer to events that happen by chance. But this encounter could not have been by chance; it was well-programmed. There was a whole episode involved, and I am sure there was a strong reason for the encounter to happen.

What else have I learned from all these events? I certainly learned to appreciate life at a different level. I learned to see doctors as messengers of God, as well as the medication, everything, and every-one-the dog, the sheep, my family, the fruit-stand vendor, even this book conveys a non-local communication. It all symbolizes the energy from the Spirit, which is faster than light, and cannot be measured.

John the Baptist saw "the Spirit of God descending like a dove and alighting Him" (Matthew 3:16). Matthew is referring to the fact that Jesus received God's blessing in the form of a dove.

Dear reader, rest and ponder.

Do you ever realize how often you are receiving non-local communications?

_____

_____

_____

Do you realize they are set up to help you see the unseen?

_____

_____

_____

Can We Change Our Models?

As we watch the world today, at the beginning of the twenty-first century, we cannot ignore the fact that ours is a dreaming universe. Consequently, we were placed on this planet to correct our dream by remembering our true reality. For that reason, we have within us a powerful energy to help undo a force of destruction called Satan.

Most of us do not see the connection between a force of destruction and a force of reconstruction.

We don't see these forces as models either. We don't see the devil as a force that sets in motion our negative emotions such as hate, anger, self-loathing, lack of love, and so forth. As we have read, his job is to tempt us; then, we have a choice to reject or not to reject.

The Bible has many examples of Satan's interference in our lives. After Jesus was baptized, He was tempted three times by the devil to convince Him to give up the Scriptures. He knew Jesus had fasted forty days and forty nights. He knew Jesus was hungry so he started to tempt Him.

> If you are the Son of God, command that
> these stones become bread.
>
> Matthew 4:3

Then the Devil took Jesus up into the holy city, set Him on the pinnacle of the temple, and said to Him, "If you are the Son of God, throw Yourself down. For it is written: 'He shall give His angels charge over you,' And, 'In their hands they shall bear you up, Lest you dash your foot against a stone."

Jesus said to him, "It is written again, You
shall not tempt the Lord your God.'

Matthew 4.5-6-7

In a third attempt, the Tempter took Jesus up on a mountain,
...and showed Him all the kingdoms of the world and
their glory. And he said to Him, "All these things I
give You if You will fall down and worship me."

Matthew 4:8-9

Of course, Jesus did not fall for any of these temptations. He always answered with quotes from God and finally told Satan to go away. And Satan did. 1 read somewhere that this is a great pattern of spiritual warfare. I believe we should keep this pattern in mind.

What is so fascinating about the Bible is that it describes and exemplifies human life as it is. For example, in the above-quoted passages, Jesus followed the script especially written for Him: it is called Salvation. But the devil also performed the job given to him, which was also scripted: and it is called temptation. These two forces, rebuilding and destruction, are part of this planet and are implanted in us as soon as we are in the womb. Since we are free to choose, it is up to all of us to decide which model to adopt.

Another very important message is described in the first sentence of Matthew 4:1. "Then Jesus was led up by the Spirit into the wilderness to be tempted by the devil"

Dear reader, I've asked you to rest and ponder several times while reading this book. Now, I ask you to write down your interpretations of the above quotes from Matthew, especially the last one.

_____

_____

_____

_____

It was Spirit that led Jesus to meet the devil in order to be tested. Do you remember how many times you have been tested? As far as I am concerned, as I look back at my beautiful life, I lost the count.

Now, I realize how successful the tempter is by making us delay our return home. I see him laughing at all the inhabitants of the earth while we don't even know how to laugh any more. We are so obsessed with our lifestyles that we don't even remember to look within ourselves.

Furthermore, we can discover from the second temptation how shrewd the devil is; he tried to convince Jesus that the angels will come and help Him if he falls down. The devil also knows the Scriptures. Do we need more proof of the importance of accepting what happened before the world began and the patterns that were made then? Do we need more proof that we can change our patterns for better or for worse? Do we need more proof that we can transform our negative thoughts to channel true Love? Do we need more proof that we are born with a very powerful energy, but most of the time we allow it to be blocked?

Jesus did not change; He is the unchanging observer. Jesus had the natural response to Satan's force of destruction-His Father. Jesus is the model for all of us.

Only we can and must change. And when we choose salvation, we will admonish the devil for his obstructions. And, of course, we'll thank God for leading us out of trouble we finally listened to His voice.

Life on this planet is wearing out; we see physical and mental deterioration everywhere. Scientists call it entropy; I call it the devil. But, as we now under-stand, there is also renewal. It is true that creation and deterioration exist everywhere, starting in our cells. It is when we go through destruction that we think of reconstruction. This is why the earth exists and why we are here, together with many forms of Satan. The earth is a laboratory.

Usually, when we reach a certain age, we start to feel our own deterioration. Like with all illusions, the good news is that they do not last long.

We've read in a previous chapter about an old man who had his face transformed and became young right after his death. His death was only physical. The great message of this event is that there is no death, but we have to die to show that. Jesus is the greatest of all examples. While we are l living on the earth, we are also in heaven. Everything is connected; our bodies are a mask, ready to be transformed at any moment to our true self. This old man had followed the models that had been imprinted in him since before the world began. Of course, like all of us, once on earth, he had not been aware of following patterns of aging, sickness, and pain.

But we don't have to wait to get old; we can start working on ourselves right now. Just remember that great non-local intelligence and energy is every-where and certainly in our DNA, waiting for our contact through our thoughts.

Throughout history mankind has endured many changes. We know that nothing in this universe is permanent and that science is speculative: what is proven today, may be disproven tomorrow. What follows is a quote from Albert Einstein, "Autobiographical Notes" (Copyright 1949):

Newton, forgive me; you found just about the only way possible in your age for a man of highest reasoning and creative power. The concepts that you created are even today still guiding our thinking in physics, although we now know that will have to be replaced by others farther removed from the sphere of immediate experience, if we aim at a profounder understanding of relationships.

This is what happened, in 1905, with Einstein's speed of light which he specified to be about 186,000 miles per second, and that nothing could go faster than that! For over one hundred years, we have been told in schools, public events, family gatherings, and so forth that one second for us moving in time, while here on earth, is equivalent to 186,000 miles in imaginary space, such as travelling to the moon.

But that was only until about the year 2000, when Dr. Wang, of Princeton University, was able to transmit a pulse of light at a speed three hundred times faster than Einstein's. Then, in 2011, scientists at CERN research center in Europe, where about ten thousand scientists work, discovered that a particle, known as neutrino, arrived at its destination 416 times faster than Einstein's. This discovery will lead to time travel! This great news was all over the media, and what happened a few days later? CERN announced that some scientists have doubts, in other words, they are not certain. It was all put on hold, until they confirm.

These two recent scientific speculations have gone nowhere, so far.

What are they afraid of? Each other? Time travel? God? And that we have to change our models which we have built in our mind and are causing so much damage to mankind?

to be made up or composed of, to be contained or inherent (Webster's Third New International Dictionary 1981).

When did we first get the idea of an atom and how? We may think it was around the nineteenth or twentieth century, and we may be surprised to find out that it actually happened about 2,500 years ago.

Two Greek philosophers, Democritus and Leucippus, arrived at the conclusion that the more they divided something, the more they realized that it could be divided no more, and they named the little piece that was left the atom. In Greek, the word atom means indivisible.

Since God does not make divisions, He made only one atom, which He shares with His Son, who created us. That is why we can say that we are one in spirit, not in body form. As long as we continue to dream that we are split, that is separated from that "energy," we are an image, a reflection, of the one atom.

Please rest and ponder.

Can you see yourself as part of one atom only, that is, an infinite energy?

_____

_____

_____

How does it feel?

_____

_____

_____

We do not know what else is in that strong force that unites all of us. In others words, the details of the elements are unknown. We even saw that when we read about the fetus in the womb that a camera could not film the beginnings of fertilization.

It is not men who will destroy us; it is our Maker who will undo the elements that He built.

No wonder Jesus said:

> Fear not, I am the first and the last, and the living
> one; I died, and behold I am alive for ever-more,
> and I have the keys to Death and Hades.
> Revelation 1:8-10, 17-18.

The Bible and Parallel Universes

In My Father's house there are many mansions.

John 14:2

Before we proceed, it is important to remember that the theory of parallel universes is still being researched; consequently nothing has been proved. However, some of the concepts, ideas, and even words are similar to what is written in the Bible. In some cases, it even seems to confirm what the Bible says. This should be no surprise since everything and everyone is connected.

It is also interesting to note that only in the past few decades physicists and mathematicians have tried to seriously investigate what happened before the big bang. As Fred A. Wolf describes in Parallel Universes (Wolf 1988), they concluded that according to new physics without parallel universes, there would have been no universe. Indeed, it is all connected now and then. We can, then, assume that neither would the Bible have been written.

New physics provides us with a new way of thinking, that is, if we let go all of our preconceived ideas which are not beneficial to us, as already referred to.

We've read that parallel universes communicate with us. We know that electrons travel; they are everywhere, and it is because of us and through us that they exist. They seem to leave us, but we never leave them. This theory should help us understand the relationship between us and the unseen, between Joseph, as described in Genesis, and his God, between Jesus and His Father.

Since we have free will, God allowed us to create many universes which manifest our dreams, wishes, and thoughts in different forms.

This is what the above quote is letting us know: In My Father's house there are many mansions (John 14:2).

Indeed, there are many roads, for which parallel universes are a symbol; they all lead to His house where there is love, light, understand, and energy.

Although we can imagine that invisible universes exist, very few of us can understand and accept the on-going communication within us which comes from what we can't see. In the chapter titled "Transformation," I refer to the story of Joseph. 1 mention how successful his prophesying was. Joseph was one of us who understood and accepted God's energy. He knew by himself he could do nothing, so he told the Pharaoh that his messages were from God, and the Pharaoh believed him. The belief of these two men made history-it changed the world. It also shows the manifestation of what is predestined, as we read in Romans 9:17,

For the Scripture says to Pharaoh, "For this very purpose I have raised you up, that I may show My power in you and that My name may be declared in all of the earth."

In this example, God gave Pharaoh a chance to choose what he had already chosen according to the Scripture.

To receive, accept, and act upon such invisible messages required that each man, and anyone else, be attuned to the energy within, and no one can do that for us, except that great intelligence, which some of us call God. All universes exist within us because they come from our Source, our Cause. As it has already been written, cause and effect are not separate. The story of Joseph is a great symbol to help us awake and understand our potential, but Jesus was the greatest contributor to such understanding.

The following quotes are from a man who was both human and divine. Because of His love for us, he chooses to be on earth to help us understand our-selves better, and our relationship with Him. In the first quote, Jesus is playing the role of a human being; although He is certain about Himself and about His father, He asks Him if He could alter His destiny.

"Father, if it is your will, take the cup away from Me;
nevertheless not My will, but Yours, be done."

Luke 22:42

Jesus knew the Father could not change what is changeless. It has been written and accomplished, so He came down to our level, to help us understand that although we are predestined, we have choices, but God has the final word.

This is exactly the way we live our daily lives-full of uncertainties, while hoping God or someone else will do everything for us. But as already mentioned, uncertainties did not exist before the big bang (Wolf 1988). On the other hand, uncertain-ties exist in this universe so that we can choose and change. The point is that we even want to change God. This concept is supported also by the next two Bible quotes.

Jesus said to Peter "Put your sword into the sheath. Shall
I not drink the cup which my Father has given me?"

John 18:11

Jesus said to one of those who were with him, "Put your sword in
its place, for all who take the sword will perish by the sword. Or
do you think that I cannot now pray to my Father, and He will
provide Me with more than twelve legions of angels? How then
could the Scriptures be fulfilled, that it must happen thus?"

Matthew 26:52-4

Relax and ponder on the two above mentioned quotes from John and Matthew, which can help us understand how much the tempter tries to convince Jesus not to follow His script and therefore change His mission.

_____

_____

_____

_____

Do you realize how much the tempter, which I also call the grand manipulator, has affected you?

_____

_____

_____

Did you choose to change, or not? Why?

_____

_____

_____

Let's have a closer look at all the quotes, in the following way:

About two thousand years ago, Jesus was remembering and acting upon a universe that represented the past but has a consequence in the future: his relationship with His father which is on-going and eternal, as per the above quote from John 18:11.

In Matthew 26:52-4, He is remembering another universe which is still attached to his choice in the past, but now represents the present and the future: his mission as our Savior.

But there was another universe in-between, which represented choices, as in Luke 22:42. All parallel universes represent choices, but some are more specific than others. We know that choices exist only while we are on earth, surrounded by uncertainties. It is here that we need to change. In the Bible, one of these universes is symbolized by a cup. We may be predestined, but we have many choices until we choose to follow the road to end it all and drink the cup which was given to us. While we are choosing, we are entertaining ourselves under hallucinations. All universes have been scripted and exist now.

Imagine yourself in a room with four video cameras containing four different movies which were scripted millions or billions of years ago, but now you see yourself in one video watching yourself in other three videos, and each represents a universe.

In one universe, you are about to be arrested and your friend Peter wants to defend you, but you stop him. Why? Because you know all there is to know: past, present, future, and in-between, but this time, and for our own sake, you are watching it in material form, in videos. You can see the universe when you promised to fulfill a mission scripted especially for you! You were certain then and forever. There is no need to choose, because it is already chosen, there is no need to change, because you are changeless. Change means doubt, and uncertainty, which, as we have read in a previous chapter, did not exist before the big bang and therefore before time.

Time is not fixed. What we think is happening now depends on the past and future. But why was Joseph's cup empty and Jesus's was not?

Joseph had already drunk his cup. He had fulfilled what had been prescribed for him as a young man: living the life of a slave in a foreign country, in his case, Egypt. Jesus, on the other hand, knew he still had to drink the cup which his Father had given him; he had yet to fulfill the script especially written for him.

Jesus never forgot the only true and eternal universe there is: His Father's. He knew He was part of that universe like all of us. And above all, He knew that He had never left.

What an extraordinary man Jesus is. What a beauty!

Rest and ponder for a moment on the following:

Have you already drunk your cup? Do you under-stand now your position in this universe? Do you understand how powerful your mind is?

Are you grateful for the energy you have been endowed with?

_____

_____

_____

How different would your life be if you had not read this book?

_____

_____

_____

Epilogue: Wake Up and Cheer

We are surrounded by a reality that we cannot see. We are surrounded by people, things, and events that do not really exist. We are certain that certainty does not exist.

We keep repeating the same models and patterns in different forms: we keep navigating among many universes. We are trying to find unity in the wrong places that is, in whatever we can measure. Can we measure love? Look at history. Wars are ongoing within us and around us. One thousand died in one day. Fifty thousand died another day.

We may kill men, but we don't kill ideas. We don't exist here; we exist in eternity, and what we are doing is following the laws that were written before the world began. We cannot say that there is nothing on this planet, because there is something that we are not able to of us. comprehend, and yet unifies all of us.

We have read that atoms do not die; our death is only physical, not spiritual.

But we have to die in order to prove that spiritual life goes on. Jesus taught that miracles are simply our return to our original condition of being one, even for only an instant. All of us are a miracle, waiting for our return and ending our entertainment, and game playing.

We keep pushing buttons to change events but the scenery is the same. Obviously, something is in charge that we cannot see neither can we control. Indeed, we are dreamers in a dreaming universe. We know that scientists too have doubts about our realities.

Insanity is everywhere. But we can learn from it. We can learn from uncertainty, entropy, our opponents, the grand manipulator, the sheep, the birds, everyone, and everything. We can learn from these reflections we are mirrors of each other.

Magic mirror on the wall, who is the Grandest Designer of all?

Selected Articles

I wrote the following articles between the year 2000 and 2006, and published them on my website. I was surprised when I read them recently and recognized how much they have influenced my writing this book. I've decided to present the articles here, after some editing. I hope you will enjoy reading them, as much as I enjoyed writing.

Time Travel and Cannibalism

Man, biologically considered, and whatever else he may be into the bargain, is simply the most formidable of all the beasts of prey, and, indeed, the only one that preys systematically on its own species.

William James

We are all cannibals, figuratively speaking. What we've done throughout history, and what we apparently will go on doing, is feed ourselves on the joys, pains, and hardships of our fellow men and women. In short, conflict is what keeps us alive.

Would it help us if we could change the past and visit the future by traveling through time? For centuries, time travel has been the dream of many people including scientists. Recently, thanks mostly to twentieth century scientists like Albert Einstein, it was announced that time travel may soon be possible.

What will time travel do for mankind? For exam-ple, you wish to buy a car. You visit the future and see that you have an accident while driving the car you just bought. You are crippled for life. Does this mean that you'll decide not to buy the car, and therefore the accident will not happen?

According to H. G. Wells, you may choose not to buy the car, however the accident will happen in some other form. In the movie Time Machine, based on a novel by the famous English writer and directed by his great-grandchild, a professor watches with horror the murder of his fiancée by a thief. He decides to build a time machine, to go back to the past, and to save her life. To his great disappointment, and in spite of the fact that he is able to change some of the events, his fiancée dies in some other accident. It seems that we are predestined. There are certain events we can change. There are others we cannot.

Disappointed with his visits to the past, the time traveler decides to visit the future. He finds himself living eight hundred thousand years from the Victorian age and discovers that there are two worlds-the upper world, and the lower world.

The upper world is populated with simple people that sometimes act like children, seem to have little or no intelligence, but can stand the light. They eat fruits and surround themselves with flowers.

The lower world is populated by strange creatures that live underground, cannot stand the light, and love machines. They also imprison the people from the upper world in order to feed themselves.

"We need their meat. How can we survive with-out their meat?" says the underground creature to the time traveler. Indeed, how can we all survive without getting fat, hungry, upset, and irritated?

Then, the underground creature goes on to say, "We can never be really free. Neither can you."

In H. G. Wells's dreams, both the upper world and lower world needs each other to prey upon.

Light and darkness are in constant conflict. This may come as a great disappointment to those of us who have hopes that science will help us to travel into the future and improve our lives.

The time traveler did exactly that, only to find out that the future is as hard and aggressive as the present. He experienced love and fear when he tried to save the woman from the cage that the under-ground people had placed her in. He experienced surprise when that same woman, from the upper world, asked him to go back to his past and take her son with him. He fainted when he saw a world of darkness. He wanted to get out and face the world, He wanted to let go of fear. Love and life became more important to him than his machine. He even wondered if the time machine ever existed, or if it was all a dream. He even asked where the dream came from.

He learned that if you want to improve your life, it is now that you must act. All knowledge is holographic and is stored within you, just like the human figure in the movie that shows up in the New York Public Library before and after it was reduced to ashes.

"I'm a compendium of all human knowledge," repeats the human figure to the time traveler. The figure appears and disappears. Sometimes it shows up in many places at the same time, other times it is nowhere. It is a reminder that in the human heart is all the answers, and that, in the end, we do not need books. All that science can do is point to our hearts.

In order to save the people in the upper world (light), the time traveler destroys the creatures in the lower world (darkness), hoping that only light will rule the world. This is the great hope of all light beings.

As the Time Traveler fought the underground creatures, they started to disintegrate. They were nothing but robots, which means that they were a product of our imagination. Darkness is our invention, a product of our dreams. Darkness is within all of us. The lower world creatures that lived in dark-ness in the underground were nothing but a mirror of us.

H. G. Wells's vision of the future shows that nothing is permanent. There cannot be change without conflict. Our role is to learn to face the world. We must fearlessly fight the enemy within the dark-ness in our minds-before it completely eats us up.

The future is now.

There Is Nothing New under the Sun

Albert Einstein must be turning in his grave.

Is there anything new under the sun? Those of us in the spiritual quest know that there isn't. Indeed, we are learning by repetition to remember what we forgot-we are all part of something beyond words, unlimited, indivisible, and instantaneous.

Plato, the Greek philosopher who lived four hundred years before Christ, wrote,

There is no such thing as teaching, only remembering. We have learned everything there is to learn, the more we seek to learn, the more we must realize that seeking and learning is all remembrance.

Meno, 79C-81A

Where does learning come from and why do we for-get? In my spiritual quest, I have learned that we are not separate from something that may be called a unified source of light, and some of us call God. I also learned why we choose to forget about our true identity and come to earth and invent symbols to help us remember.

Recently, Dr. Wang, of NEC Research Institute in Princeton, New Jersey, concluded that light arrives at its destination almost before it initiates its journey. Light seems to exist in two places at the same time, and space and time do not matter. Light, then, could carry information and cause does not seem to come after the effect. This research disrupts Einstein's work, which specifies that the speed of light (186,000 miles per second) cannot be broken. Yet, Dr. Wang was able to transmit a pulse of light at a speed 300 times faster than light. This is cause for excitement; it helps us realize that on earth, we are surrounded by nothing but symbols and metaphors that help us remember that we are part of a reality for which space and time do not matter. That reality is everywhere, therefore within us, and not just in two places. That reality knows all there is to know. It is simultaneous, therefore we never separated from it, cause and effect are not separate.

We know, deep down in our hearts, that Father/Mother (our cause) and Son/Daughter (the effect) are always together in spirit, in spite of the fact that we perceive them as separate in physical form. Scientists work with propositions to be proved later. They also work with uncertainties. The purpose of science is not to prove the existence of a higher self, for that does not need to be proven: it is continuously experienced. The purpose of science is to make our experiences seem less absurd. Indeed, all symbols and metaphors produce memory and lead to remembrance.

We know that scientists work with particles of light called photons. Photons are a symbol of unified light. Is it possible that Dr. Wang could be work-ing with something else and not light? We can rest assured that other symbols will be invented soon and will take us back to our circle of learning. We are being taught to remember again and again our real identity. Space and time do not exist. We know all there is to know; we choose to forget. This may seem hard to believe but if you think deeply it is not.

Leonardo da Vinci's manuscripts (fifteenth century) describing flying machines, launching of bombs, and scientific diagrams were considered absurd at that time. Was he more intelligent than us? No. He contacted the part of his mind where knowledge is stored. Plato did the same but as a philosopher. Bernadette, the young Frenchwoman who had mystic encounters with a beautiful lady in Lourdes, France, discovered inner peace. She later became known as a saint. You can do it too. Reflect on the following quote from Ecclesiastes 1:8, "The thing that has been, it is that which shall be; and that which is done is that which shall be done; and there is no new thing under the sun."

Within you is all the knowledge there is. Within you is all the Love and Light there is. You just for-got. Now you have to remember.

Masks and Computers

Do you know that there is a computer, at the Massachusetts Institute of Technology, still in the early stages of development that will change the way we think? In the near future, anyone who owns this computer can place it, for instance, near a politician making a very convincing speech, or next to a wife, husband, or partner who is trying to express his/her love and sincerity, and what will the computer do? It will display on the screen the truth about that person. In other words, the computer will take the mask off any individual that is not being honest and or truthful. This computer is not like a lie detector test. It is a much more sophisticated machine. It can work both for and against anyone. For instance, in the case of a person who is innocent but wants to cover up for someone else. This individual falsely testifies that he has committed a crime. Immediately the computer will say that he/she is innocent.

All of us build our own masks to suit our needs while we are on earth living in the illusion of space and time. Some of us however go to extremes. History is full of examples. There are all kinds of masks, as there are of people. One great example is Hitler. He had no formal education. He was born in Austria, and moved to Germany where he became a corporal in the army. He covered himself with such powerful masks that he was able to seduce, so to speak, the German people. He became their leader, and later one of the most horrible men in history. He made very convincing speeches, used influential words, and had great charm. He was able to switch masks to cover his true self whenever he wanted.

One day, while watching thousands of people parading in front of him, a woman placed a child on Hitler's arms. The child was about three or four years old. She was beautiful. She had long blond hair and was wearing a light blue satin dress. She smiled. Her blue eyes shined. While Hitler held her, he showed her to the crowd. The crowd got all excited and applauded with their famous "Heil Hitler" salute. Hitler kissed the child and praised all little girls as wonderful.

Some time before or after this event, Hitler visited the horrible gas chambers, where millions of people had been sent to die. They had just finished a job in one of the chambers. Hundreds of bodies were piled on the top of each other; men, women, children, and of course, beautiful little girls. All had suffocated to death. He looked through the key hole and with a sarcastic smile, walked away.

Which was the true Hitler? The one who kissed the little girl or the one who walked away with a sarcastic smile? If the German people had this computer available over fifty years ago, would they still have voted for him and kept him in power? Do you think that if the economy was good, Hitler would still be in power today in spite of what the computer would say? What would the computer display on the screen? Maybe words like cynic, liar, cheat, or even assassin, although there is no proof that he killed anyone himself.

Let's look at facts. I'm writing about masks and computers. It is a fantastic process, the way we think. We educate ourselves by allowing our false ego to build all kinds of masks around our true self. Was Hitler evil? To some he was. To others he was not. As a matter of fact, some people used to think that, without Hitler, there would be no Germany.

Yes, computers may help us to remove the masks we all cover ourselves with. Perhaps Gandhi would not have been assassinated. Perhaps Joan of Arc would not have been burned to death. Perhaps we'll become more honest with ourselves and with others. Perhaps we'll remember that our true self has no mask, and that there is a real computer within all of us the hologram. This inner computer can help us remember that we choose to cover ourselves temporarily with masks to pretend that we are what we really are not. We are afraid to show the world our true self because it is so pure, so beautiful, and so beyond words. We've allowed the false ego to teach us to be afraid of the truth. Our inner computer has all the energy and the potential to help us uncover our masks, but we find it very hard to follow the guidance that comes from within us. And so we keep building computers outside of us, and carry them anywhere we go, choosing to forget the computer within us. Hitler knew how to handle his masks in accordance with his needs in space and time. Some people say he was insane. Perhaps we are all insane. We all carry our masks. The whole world is a masquerade party. We are in a constant feast here, some-times a very painful feast.

Hitler often masquerades himself as evil. He came to earth to destroy many lives. In the end he destroyed himself. Was there a need for this? Our false ego thinks so, to the point of convincing us to join the masquerade party. Is the idea of this computer new? Of course not. I've already referred to our inner computer that gives us all the information we need, but we refuse to listen. We keep repeating our mistakes. There will be more Hitlers as long as we keep building more computers to carry around with us, forgetting the real computer that exists in everyone's mind.

Touching - Part One

Have you touched anyone today? A few weeks ago, I started to think that I'd like to write an article entitled "Touching." At that time, I had no idea how to go about it, but the title kept parading in my mind. That same week, a friend of mind called me to let me know about a great event that had just happened to her and her family.

Her mother had been hospitalized for some time with very advanced Alzheimer's. She was blind, had lost her speech, and was paralyzed. After her usual weekend visit to her mother, my friend decided to start collecting stories and write her mother's memoirs. She emailed and made phone calls all over the country to her sister, other relatives, and friends. She asked them to remember real life events, and with their help, she was able to write a few episodes. Then, she went and visited her mother.

What do you do when you visit someone who can neither see nor talk and is paralyzed? I guess you hold their hand. This is what my friend did. But, this time, as she held her mother's hand, she noticed her mother was touching hers, and was beginning to speak. Her mother, then, made an effort to raise my friend's hand and kissed it. What a surprise. What do you call this event? A miracle?

To me, there are at least two kinds of touching: physical, such as holding hands, and non-physical, which I call beyond space and time. In this case, the non-physical happened before the physical touch, When my friend started to collect the stories, she had no idea what she was going to do with them. She did not consider herself a writer and or a miracle worker. But in the end, we are all writers and miracle workers-when the time, the will, the love, and the necessity come.

So what happened during those moments when she was writing her mother's memoirs? What was communicated and how? We do not know. That is the reason why the study of modern science has been very important to me. It has helped me to accept the idea that there is a communication beyond space and time, also known as non-local, which is always going on but is, of course, invisible. We are all involved in this communication because we are the ones that trigger the button, so to speak. Without us to trigger this button so that action is activated beyond space and time, there would be no universe. Our understanding of that communication has to be very limited. We are not on earth to understand all there is. We are here to activate the button in accordance with our needs within the illusion of space and time.

Communication beyond space and time is always happening, but the individuals involved have to be ready for its manifestation. At the moment my friend started to think about writing her mother's memoirs, something touched their minds and opened up a Pandora's box, which I call forgiveness.

But not everyone is ready to forgive. As a matter of fact, I know professionals who have lost clients because they told them that they needed to forgive.

Most people do not want to forgive. They associate forgiveness with sin. I associate it with mistakes. Since we are all human, we all make mistakes. Now is the time for correction. As a catholic, I used to think that to forgive, I'd have to go and face the person that had offended me or vice versa. However, after many years of inner search, I've learned that to for-give is to remember that we are not separate-love follows. But that can only be done beyond space and time, because our memory is very limited. Somebody in my friend's family had forgotten love the writing of the memoirs contributed to the remembrance.

But who arranges all of these encounters? Who told my friend to go and collect episodes of her mother's life? There has to be a channel, what modern science calls an intelligence, a liaison, so to speak that tries to unify all things. And what a powerful intelligence it must be! We all have the potential to help each other and trigger the button that activates that intelligence, which many people call God.

Sometimes, when I'm not at my best, I remember that my life has been beautifully orchestrated, and so has yours. You may not realize it now, but wait, for it is just a question of time. Every event comes from a oneness, and everything on earth is a symbol of that oneness.

Have you ever seen the famous ballet Sleeping Beauty? People go to Lincoln Center, and or to the Bolshoi to see something extraordinary that lasts about three hours, and yet comes from a simple, short story of about one thousand words. And from that simple, short story one mind expanded and wrote beautiful music. Another mind expanded and created a beautiful ballet, and another mind learned how to dance. I think my friend did the same when she wrote her mother's memoirs. One of the stories somehow helped her mother achieve a monumental change in her mental and physical condition to the point that she started moving her hands, talking, and maybe even appreciating life again. Is my friend a miracle worker? Yes, and so are you. Do not let words impress you or put you off. Do not allow people to do that to you either. If someone tells you God does not exist or that there is no such thing as beyond space and time communication, that is

where that person is at that stage in his or her life. There may be several kinds of touching, but we are not touching alone. Jesus, for instance, while he was on earth touched many and healed many too. Some were absent healing. Today, He is not here, and yet many claimed to be healed by Him. I'm not saying that my friend is Jesus. I'm trying to say that the process is the same. Somehow, we get in touch with a thought system that we all share, and that thought can help us heal. All of us can heal even if one does not believe in God or in an intelligence. How many non-believers have been healed? They can always say, "Well, it was that medication." In the end, words do not matter. What matters is that the mission was accomplished. We all have a mission while we are here on earth, and that is to remember what we've forgotten.

To forgive, then, we do not have to face anyone but ourselves, because we've all forgotten who we really are. To remember is a monumental task. We cannot do this by ourselves. We need a Helper. That Helper is within all of us (what we call that Helper does not matter). That is why when we touch some-one, we do not touch alone, and we are really touching ourselves forgiveness is reciprocal. No one is separate. Forgiveness has to be done beyond space and time, in a realm that we cannot understand in our limited thought system, and very short memory. All we can do is accept this path as a possibility for healing, and hope for the best.

Have you touched anyone today? If you have, remember you also touched yourself.

Touching - Part Two

There are many ways you can touch somebody. How does your touching others affect you?

In my April 2001 article, entitled "Touching Part 1," I referred to my friend who was able to help her mother achieve a partial recovery from a very severe Alzheimer's condition. Since then, a few events have happened.

The whole family decided to give their mother a party at the nursing home. They read her memories. They made her listen to the music of her era. They sang, and she sang too. They kissed her, and she kissed them too. They patted her, and she smiled and cried. They were all living in the now. The hurts and fears were not remembered. Neither were the worries of the future. Only now existed. And so their mother, who had been paralyzed, speechless, and blind continued to change. She was able to touch, to feel, and to say some words.

The whole family was happy and excited. When the party was over, their enthusiasm continued. They did not want to leave the nursing home. How did they feel next day?

The daughters that had worked so hard to help their mother, and other family members, went into the greatest depression you can imagine. They could not understand what was happening. They concluded that they felt down after being so high at their mother's party. And I concluded that they had an enormous ego attack.

What is ego? The ego is that part of you that loves to harass you. It does not want you to be happy and or at peace. It does not want you to live in the now and remember true love. It wants you to constantly worry about your past and above all, the future. It wants you to feel guilty. It does not want you to learn how to handle your emotions.

It does not want you to listen to your inner voice that speaks for joy, true love, and forgiveness. The ego does not want you to remember who you really are, and that you can be at peace, even for an instant. In short, the ego is your saboteur.

But most of us do not know this. In fact, most of us are not aware of the influence of the saboteur in our lives.

I call the saboteur our thought spinner. Without this thought spinner there would be no need for the universe as we know it here on earth. Living in joy, peace, and love all the time while we are on earth is impossible. If we were always in a permanent state of joy, peace, harmony, etc., we would not need our bodies. Those of us who have read modern science know that constancy is not of this world. Everything is implicated in the other, so says American physicist, David Bohm. The good, the bad, and the ugly thoughts are always parading in our mind; and so are the thoughts of heaven and hell. An event that happened in our lives decades ago and was forgotten or buried in our thoughts suddenly pops up, and we realize we are still in pain. Yes, pain can be buried, denied, or hidden until we have decided it is time to let go of it. You do not have to have a PhD in mod-ern physics to understand life. But you need to see the world as a stage, with you playing the role of a great actor or actress.

How do actors prepare themselves for their roles?

They study their scripts intensively. You may not have a script in front of you, but you know, by now, what the ego's script looks like. Every time you have an uncomfortable thought, stop.

Whether you believe in God or not, you must realize that you can get help from within yourself. Ego's thoughts do not have power over you unless you give them power. They are not your real thoughts. Ego thoughts are not eternal. There is within you a thought system ready to help you right now if you decide to choose another road.

When my friends felt depressed after giving their mother a party at the nursing home, they did absolutely nothing to stop the ego. They did not know it was their saboteur trying to destroy their joy and the wonder of what they had accomplished. The depression went on for some time.

How do you stop your ego?

1. 1. Recognize what your uncomfortable thoughts are trying to do to you.
2. 2. Say to yourself, "You have no power over me."
3. 3. Bring the awareness to your heart. Believe it or not, you do have a heart.
4. 4. Immediately, and in accordance with your beliefs, give those uncomfortable thoughts to God, or Jesus, or the Holy Spirit, or higher self or higher intelligence. By doing this you open a new liberating road for the release of your stress.

In this world, we work with both the forces of light (a metaphor for true love, joy, peace, etc.), and the forces of darkness (a metaphor for guilt, pain, stress, fear, anger, etc.), It is a continual flux of energy. This is the thought spinner I refer to. The ego plays a major role here. We cannot get rid of the ego at this time in human history, but we can learn to recognize what it stands for and learn how to handle it.

When my friends were attending the party at the nursing home, they were living in the now. Only thoughts of joy were shared by all of them. They were in a state of euphoria-high without taking drugs. We can say that they were listening to the voice that helped them remember true love and light. This remembrance led to forgiveness and to healing without any effort on their part. This remembrance was achieved at a non-local level, therefore beyond space and time, and beyond their awareness and comprehension.

The next day, their thoughts brought them back to darkness, fear, anger, and stress. They chose to face the other side of life here on earth. Back to their jobs, apartments, conflicts, etc. Back to their ego thoughts. Everywhere you go, your mind goes with you. You can be at the beach, or anywhere else, in the most comfortable environment, and your ego thoughts will be with you. The choice is always yours. You have free will.

This is the dance of life: forces of darkness dancing around the forces of light. And why? All because we forgot who we are, and now it is necessary to remember. The Greek philosopher, Plato, in the

Republic, Book X (620), refers to each soul, passing "without looking back under the Throne of Necessity." Afterwards they went to the river of Oblivion and "every man as he drinks [forgot] everything."

We all forgot who we are; touching can help us remember. When you touch someone, you do not touch alone, and you also touch yourself. How do you handle that touching depends on your will to live in darkness or in the light, even for an instant.

Words Are Not Neutral: Are We the Victims?

The English novelist, Rudyard Kipling, once said that "Words are, of course, the most powerful drug used by mankind." Indeed, words can make you cry, can make you laugh, and can kill you. Why? Because of the images that they leave in our minds. Although most of us may not realize what is happening, such images have consequences sooner or later. Words may change from time to time, from culture to culture, from continent to continent, but something stays in our minds the effect. Can we become the victims?

Before I came to America, I had my diploma in the English language, and I had lived in England for a few years. I had met many Americans. So I thought, "Well I understand just about everything they say, but I wonder if they can understand me."

When I arrived in New York City, just about the second day, I visited the New York Public Library on 5th Avenue. I walked in and went straight to the information desk. I asked the attendant, "Miss, could you please tell me where the lift is?" She stayed

motionless, and stared at me without saying a word. I thought that she could not speak, and that maybe they hired handicapped people. I repeated the question again but to no avail. Then, I decided to make a speech, while the people behind me kept lining up and waiting. "Miss, I said, this is the second largest library in America; fifty million books, forty-eight million manuscripts and charts, beautiful architecture, and look at those lions outside. They are marble. And you do not have a lift?

She finally answered. She actually whispered to me in a nervous tone, "Non." I thought, at least, she could talk but maybe she could not hear well. So, I decided to try something new. I looked at her and said, "Miss, this is the first floor, right?" Then, I raised my right hand, pointed my thumb to the ceiling and yelled, "I want to go up, up, up."

"Ah." She answered as her body language changed. She was obviously very relieved. Then, she added, "Turn right, first left, and you'll see the elevator." It was hard to believe how much I was learning in such a short time, and I told her, "What, what? Why do you Americans, known as practical people, use such a long, Latin word elevator?" The British are certainly more practical this time because they use an easier word, lift. That was my first American-English experience.

My second experience has to do with my first date in America. Actually, it was a blind date arranged by the young man's sister, whom I had met in Europe. He was very tall, fair haired, with broad shoulders, and blue eyes. I remember holding hands with him. Since he was so tall, when he talked to me, he looked down at me while I looked up him. I do not remember where we went, but I'll never forget what he said.

"So, tell me, why did you say you came to America?" he asked.

"Oh. You know why. I came to see the United States and to visit people like your sister."

He looked at me attentively and asked me to repeat my answer. I did. Then, he added, "Oh, my dear, that is not the reason why you came to America."

I could not believe what he was saying. I thought if it was possible that this man knew more about my life than I did. I got curious and asked, "What? What are you trying to say?" He answered, "What I'm trying to say is that you came to America because of alimony and nothing else."

I had never heard the word alimony before. The English say settlement. I knew that there were divorces everywhere, including America, but I did not know that word. I had no idea what it meant, and I told him. He insisted that I knew very well what he was talking about, as I kept trying to find out what the word meant. "Oh, you mean almonds?" I asked him, as he stared at me. "It can't be almonds. You could not possibly be telling me that I came to America because of nuts. Could you please spell the word for me?"

He never spelled it, and I did not find out what alimony meant until a few days later. When some-one explained to me that it meant a settlement that usually the husbands pay their ex-wives after the divorce, I was flabbergasted.

Albert Einstein said that words are twice removed from reality. Words play no major role in the way we think. What influences us are the images the words convey. This applies to scientists and everybody else. Now, what happened to this man? By now, he has three ex-wives to support and pay alimony to. None of the ex-wives ever worked. In this story we can see the influence the word "alimony" had on this young man's mind. He carried it for years to the point that it happened in his own life.

Visiting the Empire State Building and 5th Avenue was nothing compared with the images that I still have in my mind of these events. Indeed, words are not neutral. They leave a thought or image in our mind that is imprinted for life. They have consequences. They are powerful drugs a beautiful metaphor. We may think that we are the victims.

But can we really become the victims of the images imprinted in our minds, or are we just watching the unfolding of a script that has been written? Years ago, I used to think that we were victims. However, since I started to write and do my inner search, I realized that we are not victims. How can we be victims when we choose our own path and write our own script?

There are many books, training manuals, etc. that teach that we are what we think and that we can manifest our thoughts using, for instance, affirmations. An affirmation is based on a thought that is transformed into a sentence, and if repeated over and over again, it may or may not materialize. All of us repeat affirmations, but most of the time, we are not paying attention. I think the young man that took me out on my first date in America, probably repeated throughout his life to himself and to others the word alimony until it became so ingrained in his thought system that it happened to him. He had to pay alimony not once but three times.

Big questions arise here where do our thoughts come from? Which one comes first, images or thoughts, and are they interrelated? We may not yet know the answers to these questions, but we must agree that since they play such a major role in our entire lives, they must come from a very fundamental base.

Let's contemplate the following quotes:

> The word of the Lord came to me: before I formed you in
> the womb, I knew you for my own; before you were born I
> consecrated you. I appointed you prophet to the nations.
>
> Jeremiah 1:45

Plato, the Greek philosopher who lived four hundred years before Christ, wrote in The Republic, Book X, "No destiny shall cast lots for you, but you shall choose your own destiny... The blame is for the chooser, God is blameless."

Perhaps it is easy for me to accept and to under-stand these two quotes, since I'm comfortably seated at my desk, feeling healthy and in good spirits. But what about others who may be in great stress due to a major event in their lives such as the death of a family member or a very difficult divorce? How can they accept the possibility that they have chosen the event, especially without feeling guilty?

Modern physics, or better, Quantum physics, teach us that there is no separation, and everything and everyone is implicated in the other. If intelligence, or we may say a higher self or God, participated in the formation or planning of our life prior to our arrival on earth, we too are part of that so called intelligence. As Jesus said, "My Father and I are one." He already knew about Quantum physics two thousand years ago. Our life is planned in advance. We are appointed missions before we are born and are endowed with free will. The choices are ours.

American physicist, David Bohm, spoke about the fact that Quantum energy is indivisible; observer and observed are one and the same. Separation is an illusion. He was not referring to what we can see. He was referring to what is beyond matter and yet part of us. We are not victims. We are simply watching the unfolding of the scripts of our lives that each of us wrote together with that so called intelligence. The script was written at a level that we cannot understand, at least for now, at this stage in human development. Herein lies the mystery of what we call life.

Does this mean that, for instance, a person who is going through a terrible divorce chose that particular event? The answer is yes. The choice was done when we were at a non-local level, beyond space and time and, of course, before we were born, as already referred to. At that time, we have the whole picture of our needs mapped up in front of us, but we do not have the limitations on our consciousness that we have after we are born.

I find comfort in the acceptance of these concepts, which were unknown to me until I started my inner search. It is when I'm not at my best that I appreciate these concepts the most. It is then that I tell myself; "There must be a need for me to go through this ordeal." I'm not conscious of this need now. But I'm aware that there is a part of me that knows and understands what is going on in my mind and in my life. There is always a purpose. I must have faith. You to must have faith.

But one should not be sad or disappointed about our choices which sometimes are very hard to accept.

One should really praise the person that chose to write such a script. Our short life on earth has a purpose, indeed a great and honorable purpose-to correct our erroneous thoughts of separation. The means each individual chooses to achieve that correction is not up to us to try and understand while we are in the form of matter.

In the end, then, words produce images and influence our thoughts. We invented them as we wrote the script of our lives. They stayed in our memory. When the right time comes, we'll remember them. But we are not the victims. Since we have free will, we make our choices. Be grateful and be joyous. Appreciate your courage to be here on earth in spite of the difficulties you knew you'd encounter.

To Love or Not to Love

When I was a child and living in Portugal, my father took me to see a movie about the life of Jesus Christ. Sometime during the movie, I started to think that I did not like those bad guys. I realized that they were going to hurt Jesus. So I started to yell, "Run away, Jesus. Run. Run."

My father, a nonbeliever, was very embarrassed. The more I yelled, the more he tried to calm me down, but to no avail. Everyone in the movie house was getting excited.

Finally, my father said to me, "He is more powerful than you think."

That sentence shut me up. Of course, at that time, I had no idea what my father meant, but I did not forget his words.

Only recently, I began to understand His power and the difference between real love and false love. Surely, we cannot like everyone we meet or read about or hear about. But can we love everyone?

The reasonable answer seems to be that we can-not love everyone either.

However, let's contemplate the following sentence, "There is no fear in love; but perfect love casteth out fear" (1 John 4:18).

If perfect love casts out fear, then perfect love has nothing to do with the body and fear must be out of the way. What I mean to say is that perfect love comes from spirit which is beyond the body.

Let's examine the reason why I did not like those bad guys in the movie. True, I was a child, but my ego was big enough to fear what those bad guys would do to Jesus. How interesting it is to realize how we grow up fearing and disliking the bad and the ugly.

What happens to love? We are taught to love the good, the kind, and the gentle. In the end, what we are learning is the concept of separation, which can never inspire true love, because true love comes from a unified source, and that never changes.

The concept of separation, however, is the basis for our illusory existence on earth. Are we being helped by such a concept, or does it become a hindrance as we grow up? Can we learn to love without the concept of separation?

The answers to these questions are settled deep in our thought system. We already know the answers, but we ignore them. As we grow up, we begin to understand that the ego is a hindrance because it tries to prevent us from looking within and discovering that the light in us is more powerful than the darkness. This is the power of true love. The ego tries to prevent us from seeing ourselves as we really are an eternal light. In a nutshell, the ego, being the thought of separation itself, keeps itself alive by constantly hiding the truth from us, and perpetuating our discomforts.

Love, I mean real love, is beyond the concept of separation. It has nothing to do with the body or with what we can see or touch. The ego has to be out of the way because there can be no fear, no anger, no expectation-in short, no conditions.

My father was in a nursing home for four years. There was another man there, much younger than my father, whose wife used to visit him only to quarrel with him. Sometimes, she even beat him up with his cane. One day, my father and I were playing Dominos; she was so close to us that she almost hit us. I tried to talk to her husband to see if I could make him feel better, without really knowing how he was feeling. He listened to me for just a few seconds, and then said, "Miss, she is a good wife. She has always been a good wife."

We all choose different ways to express our problems our need to be truly loved. I call these ways forms. In this case, the wife chooses to beat up her husband. Her husband, on the other hand, chose to stay with her and accept her actions. I'm not suggesting that if you truly love someone, you have to stay with that person and accept whatever it is he or she wants to do to you. What I'm saying is that you have choices. You can always say "I love you, but I'm leaving. Thank you for the experience."

> You have the power to choose the forms you
> want to use to express yourself. You have the
> power to express your needs in a loving way, or in

a non-loving way. The choices are yours and so are
the consequences.

As children, we have to learn about fear and how to protect our body. In short, we need to build a healthy ego. As adults, we have to learn to see beyond the body-beyond the thought of separation. In other words, we have to understand that we live in two worlds. One is illusory and temporary (ego); the other is real, never changes, and is eternal. This concept makes life very interesting and even mysterious.

Where do the thoughts of perfect love come from? They do not have to come from anywhere because they exist within you. You received perfect love before you were born; therefore, it is within you and will always be. In truth, you do not need to learn how to love. Believe it or not you are love. Only the ego tries to show you that you need to learn how to love. Only the ego tries to show you that love is apart from you, and therefore, you have to go and look for it.

When I was growing up in Lisbon, I had a friend who had two sisters. Her mother worried about her because she liked to stay home, while her sisters went out a lot dancing, etc. Her mother used to ask me, "How is she going to find someone to love her and marry her if she is always home?" Obviously, I did not know how to answer.

Their apartment was on the first floor of a building near my house. I never had problems visiting her because I knew that every afternoon she used to open the window of her bedroom, contemplating the people that went by. Sometimes, she'd exchange a greeting with the passers-by. And so we used to talk for hours. I was outside on the street. She was inside in her apartment.

What happened to these three sisters? One never married. One married and divorced. My friend married. As far as I know, she is still happily married to the same man. How did they meet? Right there where she used to be every afternoon.

We all know we are on earth temporarily. What we do not remember is that this is our chance to allow perfect love to express and expand itself. This is where most of us get in trouble. In our desperate need to show who we really are a lovely light-we stumble. Most of the time, we choose the wrong forms to express our needs. We allow our thoughts of separation to take over our precious lives.

The ego teaches us that we have to like someone in order to love this person; this is one of its conditions. This is false love. Perfect love is beyond liking. You may not like someone, yet deep down, you always love this person, even if you are not aware of it now, and even if you do not understand how that is possible. True love is not to be understood; it is to be experienced. It is to be enjoyed.

Sometimes I used to plan a few sentences to tell my father how much I loved him whenever I visited him in the nursing home. I had the sentences in my mind for days, sometimes for months. But once I got to visit him, all I did was to play Dominos with him. There was no need for words. There was no need for affirmations. We were both at peace. At times, it was so peaceful that we even forgot the time for his dinner. The message had been conveyed beyond words and, somehow, beyond space and time. My body was not needed to convey the message, neither were my words. Only my thoughts were necessary. Is this communication from God or science or spirit? Does it really matter to investigate where it is from?

What about Jesus? Why does history portray him in this fashion? Jesus's thoughts were beyond liking and beyond the ego's thoughts of separation. Therefore, Jesus's thoughts were beyond false love. Only thoughts of true love occupied His mind. Again, there was no condition. That was His mission; that was the form he chose while he was here on earth.

So Jesus did not run like I wanted Him to. If He had run, then He'd be following his ego thoughts that were commanding Him to fear what was going to happen to Him. And yes, He had tremendous power, as my father said. His power was totally invisible. It was the power of the mind. The power that reminds us that true love does not come from anything outside of us, but it is totally subjective.

You do not have to learn how to express true love. You are that expression. You are the receiver and the giver. You are that unconditional love that you so desperately search for.

Time

That which is, has been; that which is to be, has already been; and God seeks what has been driven away.

Ecclesiastics 3:15

Imagine a universe so hot that nothing moved. All was still. There was only one single force. As that force cooled off, it started to split. Movement was initiated a particle was born. Scientists named it time.

But they are not sure if time was the first particle. The split and formation of the first particle caused other particles to be formed. They were named height, length, and breadth. This was the beginning of what scientists call a real universe.

As time passed, they realized there are more dimensions-all entangled, all very, very small. They hope these dimensions will help them put together a theory that unifies everything. In the meantime, physicists are trying to find the answers to two questions: Was time the first particle to be formed? And what was that single force that caused it?

It is possible that, with time, they may find some answers, but in a limited way. These answers will be nothing but a symbol for a much higher reality. Scientists are counting on the help that high-energy colliders also known as accelerators can provide them. These colliders can create temperatures simi-lar to what physicists imagine existed at the time of the first split.

In the end, the ultimate answers are always within each individual and not in what they build outside of themselves. Only the mind has the unlimited potential to create or to miscreate.

That is why time was invented. Time, then, is a tool that we've been given to see how we handle our thoughts. Do we look within, or do we look outside of ourselves? And yes, time is a temporary tool. I've learned, in my spiritual quest, that time and space will eventually disappear. Now, even physicists agree.

Let's do the best we can to use time constructively and hopefully live a peaceful and healthy life.

Are you using your time constructively?

Why do some of us survive pain, stress, fear, etc., while others perish?

I've watched people change practically overnight from young to old, their dark hair turned white, all because of a major problem they have to face.

History has many examples. Alexander Solzhenitsyn, a concentration camp survivor, wrote about his experiences as a political prisoner in his own country-Russia. Anatoly Shcharansky also wrote about his experiences as a Russian Jew who survived years of imprisonment and torture by the KGB, also in Russia. Victor E. Frankl, a holocaust survivor, describes in his writings how some perished while others survived and even grew while in Nazi prisons. These are examples of people who survived pain.

All of us are part of history. All of us use time all the time and allow our minds to build our own prisons or to set us free. We use time to hate, to fear, to kill, to love, etc. We may even use time to investigate the mysteries of the birth of time. We may use time to heal. We may use time to see if we can understand our relationships and, above all, to see if we can handle fear, anger, pain, stress, etc.

But the most constructive use of time is when we try to experience our relationship with our inner self. That moment is precious because it contains all the information there is, all the truth about you. That moment is also rare because we choose, most of the time, to look outside of ourselves for answers.

When Albert Einstein began to discern an unseen and powerful force in the universe he named it cosmological constant. It baffled him so much that he put it aside.

Today scientists thank Einstein for his work. Research is now showing that the universe is expanding so rapidly that soon there will be nothing to see but us. Space and time will not survive; they are illusions. You are beyond illusions; you are eternal.

All galaxies-forms of matter will not be seen. But, we'll see ourselves because we are beyond mat-ter. The universe is infinite; matter is not.

You are the universe. You are the ultimate reality. You are both the observer and the observed. Within you is all there is.

The distinction between past, present[,] and future is only an illusion, however persistent.

Albert Einstein 1879-1955; letters to Michelangelo Besso, March 1955

In the end, you must remember that there is a powerful, invisible force everywhere, and that means within you. That powerful force will keep you alive, independent of the form you choose to mask your-self with.

You are the absolute ruler of yourself. How successfully you rule yourself depends on how often you use time constructively.

Artist of Life

The artist is not a special kind of man, but every man is a special kind of artist.

Ananda Coomaraswamy, 1877-1947, Transformation of Nature in Art (1934)

Do you think only famous people like Michelangelo and Leonardo da Vinci are artists? Praise yourself, for you are an artist too. Some people build monumental works that are remembered forever. But how do they sculpt their own lives?

Indeed, life is an art. You are your own sculptor. You are not separate from the sculpture. As with all other artists, the sculpture that you make is an expression of your own thoughts-a manifestation in form. You do not see the thoughts. You are limited to seeing only the forms. However, more important than the forms are, certainly, your thoughts.

If you have thoughts of joy, peace, good health, then you realize you're surrounded by true abundance which can help you build the greatest work of art-your life.

How do you sculpt your life? Why is it easier to sculpt for some of us than others?

Saul Bellow wrote,

I feel that art has something to do with the achievement of stillness
in the midst of chaos. A stillness which characterizes prayer,
too, and the eye of the storm. I think that art has some-thing
to do with the arrest of attention in the midst of distraction.

George Plimpton, Writers at Work, 1967

All of us share the need to still our minds. But not all of us are
able to achieve such stillness, especially in the midst of turmoil. This
is the core of the artistry of life.

Think of your life as a garden. Have you ever tried to cultivate
your own garden? Is it easy or difficult? Whether it is indoors or
outdoors, you need, at least, planting soil, seeds, and water. You need
also patience, dedication, and concentration. Above all, you need to
remove all the blocks that are preventing you from cultivating your
garden. Thoughts of fear, hate, anger, and even stress have to be out
of the way, for this is the kind of distraction that prevents you from
sculpturing your life in a peaceful and loving way.

Extra patience may be necessary. You must try, again and again, to
let go of all the thoughts that prevent you from planting your garden.
You may wonder where your thoughts come from. Painful thoughts can
come only from your lower self, whereas joyous and loving thoughts
can come only from your higher self.

How can you remove the thoughts that you do not want? First you
need a point of reference and an image. The point of reference is your
heart; the image is the ray of light that exists within you.

It is a privilege to be living at a time when science confirms what
mystics, philosophers, and others have been saying all along-light is
everywhere and, therefore, within you.

Whether you pray to God, Jesus, Allah, Buddha, or the Sun, or
even if you do not pray at all, it is important that you recognize that
you have a heart and that you are a beautiful ray of light. What you
call that light, it does not matter.

Consequently, bring your awareness to your heart. If possible, place your hand on it. Close your eyes. Remember the light within you. Imagine a beautiful ray, and choose a bright color or even a rainbow. Ask to let go of thoughts of fear, anger, stress, etc., that are preventing you from cultivating your gar-den. Then, concentrate on your heart and the ray of light. How long you hold on to this concentration is up to you. However, let me assure you that if you achieve an instant of peace, you are already a winner.

Your garden will bloom eternally and so will your trees, plants, and bushes. An abundant harvest will follow. Be grateful for who you are and for your achievements; they will be admired by many that you cannot see or hear.

Now you know how to become an artist of life.

To Kill a Body

To kill is to destroy life. Can life really be destroyed? In my spiritual quest, I've learned that a body is

a frame which tries to hide hate, fear, anger, guilt, false love, and, certainly, spirit. We can make the frame disappear, but not the content. This is another way of saying that ideas and thoughts come from a source beyond the body, and therefore undergo constant recycling. One life affects another life and another and another. American scientist, David Bohm, called this recycling "The Implicate Order."

This concept brings up an important question: What makes us human? Is it the frame, called the body, or is it the constant recycling of ideas and thoughts?

Those of us who have seen movies such as Beauty and the Beast and The Hunchback of Notre Dame know how disfigured the beast and the hunchback look. But then, as their stories of love and under-standing unfold, we change our minds. We forget about their looks. We see them as human.

There are animals who behave like humans. There are humans who behave like animals. It is all relative. The worst criminal on earth has been called a wonderful human being by his family.

It is an illusion to think that we can get rid of the content by making the frame disappear. Jesus Christ is, certainly, a great example. His life in bodily form was short. His life as Spirit is eternal. We are surrounded by illusions. Everything around us is a symbol of a much higher reality.

It seems that we are in desperate need of a new metaphor that will help us understand what it means to be human.

So many people worry about the disappearance of the human race by natural disasters, or other means. Atlantis, a continent that existed in the area known today as the Atlantic Ocean, disappeared into the sea thousands of years ago. Plato and other authors wrote about it. But then, they say it is a legend. There are pyramids in Central America, the origins of which are unknown. Who built them? Where did these builders go?

All of us are afraid to be stripped of our frame. We fear there will be nothing to look at but the con-tent, and most of us do not want to look inwardly. We find it painful to look at illusions, thinking they are reality. We also find it painful to realize that, in the end, there is nothing to fear our true self is beyond any frame and content.

Where would ideas and thoughts go if the human race disappears? Ideas and thoughts do not need our bodies to exist. They do not need human bacteria either. The same source that implants them in us implants them in other frames such as birds, plants animals, robots, and others we've yet to find out.

Robots are, at present, laughed at. Soon, they will be feared and hated. We do not believe that robots can be as or as perfect intelligent as we are. But this is not what computer scientists think. They believe that robot intelligence will surpass ours in this century.

I used to think that my nose was not only beautiful, but also useful; that was until I read the latest robot-nose news. I learned that there are advanced electronic noses that smell illness. But this is not all. In 1977, a computer named Deep Blue beat chess champion Gary Kasparov. Another program com-poses music.

How can this be? How can a machine know the steps to play chess and have the thoughts, feelings, and emotions to compose music?

The recycling goes on. Everything in the universe is in constant motion. We've learned from modern physics that all material things are connected at a level that we cannot understand. Everything is made up of particles that communicate with each other.

Until last century, only saints were supposed to have light around them. This is the type of light that cannot be seen with the human eye. It is the type of light that means power of thought, strength, and energy of unknown sources. Only some artists, who were also visionaries, were able to paint such images. But, then, Kirlian photography was discovered. Now, we can see this invisible light around every individual, every object, every bird, every tree, etc.

If computers are programmed by humans, so are we programmed by genes, chromosomes, the world around us, and much more that we will have to find out. You can destroy a frame, but you cannot destroy ideas and thoughts. Above all, you cannot destroy spirit, which makes life eternal and is the universal force.

> The man who was made in God's image is the inner
> man, the incorporeal, incorruptible, immortal one.
>   Origen (185-254) Holimy on Genesis

All frames are to be respected. Whatever frame you are in right now, love and respect it. The human body needs good care. It is like a garden. It needs to be carefully planted, watered, and watched over. Never forget to cultivate your garden and to allow your neighbors to cultivate theirs with love, tender-ness, understanding, and appreciation.

Oneness will always exist. Oneness is immortal and beyond intelligence.

E.T. The Extra-Terrestrial, We Need You.

How can a fatherless boy be comforted by a wrinkled puppet?

At first sight, there was nothing physically attractive in this puppet. As a matter of fact, his appearance scared everyone, including the little boy, Elliott, who played the major role in the movie E.T.

E.T. features extra-terrestrials, but, in the end, the movie is not just about an extra-terrestrial who wants to go back home; it is about all of us in our inner search for our true home and our true Father.

The movie has many universal symbols of love, healing, and communication. Seeing E.T. over and over again, as I did twenty years ago and now, it is like taking a crash course in the importance of understanding and accepting a form of communication which is too often invisible, hardly noticed, and rarely appreciated by most of us. We are all very impressed as we watch the characters in the movie communicate; but we never ask ourselves how this communication is possible or where it comes from.

At the beginning, unaware of E.T.'s presence, Elliott threw candy into his backyard, wondering if a coyote was hiding somewhere. E.T. collected all the candy, and surprised Elliott, later on, as he gave the candy back to him. Elliott realized he had good company. From that time on, he realized he had someone to share his life with. He began to understand that "to give is to receive." This was the beginning of their friendship. Elliott was no longer scared of his friend's looks.

At the end of the movie, Elliott's sister, in tears, kissed E.T. while Elliott, also in tears, gave him a long embrace. Separation is not easy. Elliott wanted E.T. to stay on earth with him, but E.T. kept repeating the sentence, "Go Home." He even suggested that to the devil played by another child in the Halloween party scene in the movie. I cheered this short episode when I first saw the movie twenty years ago. At that time, my education had convinced me that the devil was a heavy male figure with two horns on his head. He was separate from me. Consequently I thought that if I could kill or destroy him, I'd have peace of mind. But by now, I've learned that the devil is within all of us. When we die, we either take him with us or not.

The devil is a great symbol for that part of our thought system that causes anger, hate, fear, guilt, and separation. If, while on earth, we learn how to handle the devil in us, we can have genuine peace here and now; for home is here, there, and everywhere.

We've learned to respect our environment, to take care of trees, birds, animals, water, but we've yet to learn to love and respect ourselves and others. Above all, we've yet to learn to listen to our inner self, and appreciate the communication that exists within all of us. Albert Einstein and other dedicated individuals some called saints, some called scientists-worked very hard at trying to understand and even explain this type of communication.

It is obvious that E.T. communicated through Elliott, but it is not obvious how this communication happened. Herein lies the mystery of life a great way to remind ourselves that our higher self, God, and the Holy Spirit also communicate through us.

While Elliott was at school, E.T. drank too many drinks from his friend's refrigerator. He got sick, burped, and collapsed. The same thing happened to Elliott except he was not drinking; he was sitting at his desk. The teacher called his mother to say that Elliott was intoxicated.

In another scene, E.T. learned to switch on the TV. He watched a couple kissing. Immediately, Elliott, still in school, grabbed one of his school-mates and kissed her.

Intrigued by where the extra-terrestrial came from, Elliot and his siblings showed him maps of the planets, including the earth. He looked at these maps with curiosity. Then, he pointed his long skinny finger to the sky and said home. Suddenly, a table in the room started to shake, and the planets (small balls) jumped out of the map and started to float around the room; a symbol of the lack of reality and permanence of the universe.

There are also calls for freedom-free the frogs, free E.T., in the end, free all of us from pain, stress, loneliness, and, above all, the thought of separation.

"You have absolute power," says Elliott.

Indeed, you have the power to hate and to fear, but you also have the power to love and to heal. That power can come only from within you in the form of light shared by everyone.

A beam of light from E.T.'s finger completely healed Elliott's bleeding finger. E.T.'s heart, too, is a great symbol of love. A deep red flame glows and completely illuminates his chest-a symbol of Christianity's sacred flame.

Is E.T. fiction or nonfiction? It seems that we are on the verge of great changes in our thought system. In a recent BBC article, we are told that the US army has selected Massachusetts Institute of Technology (MIT) in Boston to create robo-soldiers-human beings that will jump buildings, heal themselves, and even become invisible. Special uniforms will protect the soldiers from bullets, and they may even be able to activate offensive weapons. Special shoes will release super strength and energy. Welcome to a new world of fiction.

When E.T., Elliott, and his friends went on a wild bicycle ride fleeing from the authorities who were after the extra-terrestrial, they must have also wondered where that power came from. What made their bicycles fly over trees, houses, and mountains?

When E.T. was about to die, Elliott was very sick too. E.T. died, but Elliott's thoughts separated from his friend's; he recovered his energy and went on living.

Then, Elliott, thinking E.T. was dead, said to him, "I love you." Suddenly, the extra-terrestrial resurrected, and at the same time, the withered flowers on a flower pot came back to life. These are all great symbols of our inner strength, communication, and, above all, eternal life which is supported by true love.

In the end, E.T. went home with the help of his little friends from the earth, but not until his fin-ger pointed to Elliott's lips and he said, "Ouch." A reminder to all of us that life hurts.

Then, in his final good-bye, E.T. pointed towards the top Elliott's of head and said, "I'll be right there." This is a great reminder that true love never leaves you. It is your mission to remember; that's why we need movies like E.T.

The final image in the movie is a rainbow, a symbol of our connection to our higher self. The extra-terrestrial, Elliott, and all of us will eventually go back home to our Father, and realize that we never left for there is a rainbow within all of us.

The Sound of Music, Then and Now

What is music?

> Music is your own experiences, Your thoughts, your wisdom.
> If you don't live it, it won't come out of your horn.
> Charlie Parker 1920-1955

In the movie The Sound of Music (1965), the Reverend Mother told Maria she has a great capacity to love but has to find out how God wants her "to spend her love."

Maria is shocked, fearful, and confused.

Who is Maria? In real life, she is the English actress Julie Andrews; in the movie she plays the role of a nun in search of her true self.

"I've pledged all my life to His service," said Maria to the Reverend Mother.

Maria loved God, how could she possibly love her boss, Captain Von Trapp, too? Like many of us, Maria thought love had limits. It was the Reverend Mother who reminded her that true love between two people is also holy; when you love someone, "it does not mean you love God less. Furthermore, an Abbey is not a place to be used as refuge for those who do not want to face their problems."

Maria was also a happy young nun who occasion ally ran away from the Abbey to the hills nearby to sing and dance. She knew there was another world out there beyond the Abbey's walls, but she feared the change.

At first, she pleaded with the Reverend Mother not to send her away to face the man she loved but, in the end, she changed her mind after listening to her sounds of music:

Climb every mountain Follow every stream

We all write our own music, and sing it in different forms. In order to do this, all doors must be opened and fear must be out of the way. We must allow our higher self to guide us.

What is to reach the heart must come from above, if it does not come thence, it will be nothing but notes-body without spirit.

Beethoven, to J. A. Stumpff, 1824 in Marion Scott, Beethoven

Maria married the captain, and became an instant stepmother of seven children: a true story that happened in Austria just before World War II. From the moment she married, Maria's sounds of music changed drastically. She had to face not only her new love but also the Nazis' hate.

When they came back from their honeymoon, they were surprised to see the Austrian flag, at the entrance of their mansion, replaced by the Nazis flag. Captain Von Trapp tore it to pieces. Convinced that there was no more free Austria, the family refused to let the Nazis take control of their lives. With courage and commitment, they escaped to Switzerland, but not before the whole family sang, "God bless my homeland forever."

We've learned that history repeats itself. Is this type of sound of music a sign of historical events about to happen again in the twenty-first century?

Which flags will be replaced?

Let's follow our rainbows until we find our dreams and hopefully escape the rage of evil. After all, that is what miracles are all about.

Civilization: What Is It?

Civilization will begin when the power of love replaces the love of power.

A journalist asked, "Mr. Gandhi, what do you think of modern civilization?"

Mr. Gandhi said, "That would be a good idea."

Is civilization a work in progress in everyone's mind or just an idea that will never materialize? No one refers to civilization as good or bad. We refer instead to primitive versus advanced civilizations, implying that there is progress.

Recently, I was invited by a family from another culture to attend a special event. After the food was served, I waited for the forks, knives, and spoons, but they never arrived. Then, I noticed everyone eat-ing with their fingers. I did the same. I've not had such an experience since I was a baby. I did not miss the silverware. I admired those people, especially the women. They have suffered so much abuse in their countries-civil war, starvation, family separation, loss of family members, and slavery. But the women smile. They look beautiful. Is it because they are now in America, or because someone taught them the power of love instead of the love of power? These people are the real winners because they conquered

the enemy within themselves. Children are born without culture. In primitive Societies, the environment was the classroom. There was no rush. There was no time. What changed their activities were the sunset and the sunrise which they admired greatly. Their thoughts were turned inwardly.

A stone-age man confronted with a watch may have thought he was having a dream. A modern-age man confronted with cannibalism may think he is having a nightmare. Yet, the watch and cannibalism exist in space and time.

In Papua, New Guinea, laws forbidding cannibalism were implemented late in the twentieth century. Cannibalism, however, was practiced recently.

In Russia, a three-dimensional map carved in thick stone and buried under the ground was recently discovered to be 120 million years old. Only a very advanced civilization could have built such a map.

When the Romans and the Arabs invaded Lisbon, Portugal, they were fascinated not only by the climate and the landscape, but also by the abundance of fresh, clean, pure water. Today, there is only one fountain in the old district. If you are not near that fountain, you have to pay at least one dollar for a bottle of water which usually comes from other parts of the country.

We've allowed technology to enslave our bodies and our minds. We've turned our thoughts outward to machines and to concrete, instead of inwards to our hearts and our right mind.

We cannot stop the advances of technology. We can, however, stop hurting ourselves by learning to look inwardly. It is never too late. The only time there is, is now.

The progress of civilization can only be the progress of people's minds towards civility, politeness, and an understanding of who we really are. It is an ongoing process, and it happens independently of space and time.

A person in the twenty-first century may show no signs of being more civilized than a primitive person. There are very powerful tribal rituals happening right now in many cultures. For instance, a man cuts his legs and lets them bleed for a while in order to celebrate a special event. He stands still and motionlessly with his arms and legs crossed over his chest. He shows no signs of pain or discomfort. He learned to control his mind to think beyond his body. He is at peace during the whole event. We, in our advanced society, cringe when confronted with these events. We may even feel pain just watching them on TV. Our culture has not helped us to train our minds to think beyond our bodies and to learn to be at peace.

The value of civilization is not in a new missile that travels five thousand miles; it is in the way we handle our thoughts not only for the benefit of each individual, but also for the whole, because the whole is in every part. This concept may seem hard to understand. You do not have to understand, you just have to accept that there is an invisible communication that unites all there is.

For some of you, these ideas may be classified as religion. For others, these ideas may be classified as modern science such as physics. In the end, neither of these are important. What really matters is to understand and accept that we are free to see that the power of love is more powerful than the love of power.

The Apes

I always wanted to visit Gibraltar. I was intrigued by the pictures of this big rock surrounded by water and flat land in the southern tip of Spain.

I was surprised to find a lot more to see than just a rock. Also known as the Pillars of Hercules, the Rock of Gibraltar conveys a powerful image of strength-not to mention its strategic location. It is the closest point between Europe and Africa; on a clear day, we can see the African Continent across the Mediterranean.

I stared at the rock with awe, especially when I found out that about two hundred million years ago, the rock was under the sea.

What happened? Was it global warming that caused such a change? Was it the power of nature or intelligent design or God?

Perhaps it is not as important to find out the cause as it is to realize that, although the world around us changes, our basic needs do not. To this day, shelter, food, love, and understanding are most important to our survival. Somehow we are born with enough intelligence or intuition to fend for ourselves. Our surroundings are also built in a way to supply us with our needs. But what about love?

Gibraltar was inhabited by prehistoric men and women who lived in prehistoric caves, such as St. Michael. Perhaps, the most dramatic natural grotto in Europe, St. Michael has an underground lake, and to visit parts of this grotto, the visitors have to climb a rope.

There are also many miles of underground tunnels. Here, General Eisenhower planned the invasion of North Africa during the Second World War. The Muslim invasion of Europe started here in the fifth century Ad as well.

There are wild trees and birds, nature walks, and dolphin watching. But, more important than any of these is the compassionate expression of the tailless Barbary apes that occupy part of the rock and roam free. They let themselves be photographed next to us; they defy the drivers and place themselves on the top of cars, jump on the window sills, and show up everywhere. They carry their babies, feed them, and groom each other with pride. They are having fun. Above all, they are confident no one will hurt them. They are able to stand still and stare at us for some time. Indeed, in their contemplation of human beings, the apes are reminding us of what they have done for themselves they have freed themselves from the chains and the stress of the jungle. Have we freed ourselves from the chains we've built around us and within us?

A man doesn't learn
To understand anything unless he loves it.

Goethe

What is love? In my short life on earth, I've learned that love and understanding are interconnected. We must first understand ourselves, then, we'll under-stand and love others. This does not mean that we have to go through some intense intellectual training. On the other hand, this understanding must be effortlessly achieved.

We all know that science has been teaching that all thoughts are interconnected. Scientists explain this interconnectedness in terms of photons, electrons, atoms, and other components. Spirituality teaches the same, except our interconnectedness is beyond photons, electrons, and atoms. Our short life on earth is our choice and responsibility. We not only choose to come here, but we also come with a well written script that will help us expand our horizons and grow spirituality.

Did you ever wonder about the similarity of your thoughts and the apes'?

Are you sending thoughts to the apes, or are they sending them to you? Or are you simply sharing the same thoughts? Do the apes understand us better than we understand them? Did you ever question the fact that your thoughts come from a source beyond your body? What makes you think? Are you thinking at all?

Imagine yourself writing a play. You choose the characters, the settings, and the plot. Then, the actors go on stage and follow the written script. Whether you like it or not, whether you believe it or not, you are doing the same thing every day of your life. The difference is that you are not conscious of the script.

And this is what makes life so mysterious.

If you accept the idea of the script, then you are ready to achieve inner peace. You can begin to under-stand that there is a purpose for every event in your life and everyone you meet. You start to let go of emotions such as anger, fear, and hate. You begin to let go of the characters that show up in your life and somehow upset you. This is also the road to forgive-ness. Every time you are going through hell, remember that you can achieve inner peace. The power of choice is yours.

Now you can let go of the chains of ignorance that you built in your mind. You can begin to love yourself and others.

Rest in Peace

Peace, Rest, and Bliss dwell only where
there is no where and no when.

Arthur Schopenhauer

When I was a child, my mother took me to visit my grandfather's graveyard.

"Grandpa is not dead," I said to her. She seemed surprised. She took my hand and walked me away from the burial site.

"What did you say?" she asked.

"Didn't you read the words on that big stone 'Rest in Peace'? Grandpa can't be dead," I insisted. "We are still talking to him; we are wishing him well."

She seemed a bit shaken by my observations. She tried to convince me that he was definitely dead, but I did not believe her. It was only recently that I began to understand how much we fear the thought of eternity and true love.

To rest means to be awake, to be totally aware of who we really are. When we are at peace, we are alive; we are aware that we are not separate from a unified thought system. We may not even be conscious of this wholeness. But deep down within us, we've calmed down and switched our perception from being alone and separate to being united and whole.

Being dead means nothing; it is our greatest illusion and needs to be corrected. How do you achieve this correction? Do you need religion or science or a politician to show you the way? You may think you need all of the above. But, in the end, you are the ultimate source of information.

Every day of your life is a lesson on who you are. You may choose to be a doctor, a taxi driver, a housewife, and so forth until you realize that your real profession is to be a student of life.

The sentence, "Rest in Peace," should be repeated silently by each of us, as often as possible, especially during busy and painful times. Our interior dialogue is a constant war from which we desperately battle to free ourselves, from whatever thoughts are disturbing our peace.

Where does the idea of freedom come from? Certainly, our thoughts do not come from out there. Manhattan, for instance, exists because we built it. Our minds choose the road to follow. We are endowed with free will.

Many of us do things in this world because society tells us so. We torture ourselves with relation-ships we don't want because we think we need them. Once, I met a woman who told me she had to have children because all her friends had kids.

Our internal war will go on until we realize we have to free ourselves from fear, hate, anger, guilt, and, above all, false love.

We have to put ourselves in the other person's shoes, so to speak. We have to see that all of us are in the same boat. This does not mean that we let others step on us. We have to learn to understand that in the end, all of us are desperately searching for true love. This is our mission while here on earth. It is this understanding that frees us from the fear of eternity. What is true cannot be found out there; it can only exist within us and never goes away-we simply forget. There are two kinds of peace-inner and outer.

> Mine is a policy of peace.
>
> Benito Mussolini

> What a beautiful fix we are in now: peace has been declared.
>
> Napoleon Bonaparte

> Peace cannot be kept by force. It can only
> be achieved by understanding.
>
> Albert Einstein

The first two quotes refer to fake peace a peace in the world outside our minds the kind of peace that is imposed by others. The quote from Einstein can be interpreted both ways. We all know what happened to Mussolini and Napoleon, but we've yet to realize how much damage we do to ourselves by not understanding who we really are. Since the thought of war begins in our minds, it is in our minds that peace must be built.

Everyone we encounter provides us with a les-son in the art of living. You may decide to divorce your wife or husband or change jobs, but are you really free? Was that separation done with true love and understanding? Did you ask your inner self to help you?

We've been trained to see the world, and therefore, our problems out there. As long as we do not solve the problems in our mind, there will always be wars out there; they are a reflection of the war going on within us.

War, Peace, and Potatoes

> Nothing can bring you peace but yourself.
>
> Ralph Waldo Emerson

One of the most interesting events in my life was to volunteer at Covenant House in New York City, an institution to help runaway teenagers.

My main task was to serve dinner. I was given about 150 big, fat potatoes and asked to distribute one potato to each resident, except pregnant women or individuals with children they would get two potatoes. I had to count the potatoes as I gave them out and inform the supervisor of the total count.

At the beginning, I had no idea how much the potatoes would stir my emotions. Gradually, I started to wake up during the night dreaming of potatoes-counting potatoes, drowning in potatoes, and fighting potatoes, even with my fists. These images repeated themselves in the morning, afternoon, and evening until I started to serve potatoes again. They became my inner enemy. I was at war with potatoes.

How dare those big, fat potatoes interfere with my usually peaceful state of mind? By the same token, how dare I allow such interference?

How perilous it is to free a people who prefer slavery.

Machiavelli

After some deep thinking, I realized the potatoes were a symbol I had chosen to express the anger I felt within myself. I was angry at the parents of those teenagers for not loving them. I was also angry at some of the teenagers for not loving their parents. I was even angry at myself as I questioned my relationship with my parents.

Indeed, we project our inner thoughts in what we think is the world out there when, in truth, the problems are within us. We all do this projection in different forms. I chose potatoes to fight the war within me, whereas another individual may choose, for instance, to commit a crime, therefore, allowing his or her anger to go to extremes. Then, we say that there is evil in this world.

Beware, evil is not in this world but within us. I'm not saying that we are all like Hitler, Stalin, or Blue Beard. What I'm saying is that we all project our thoughts outward, in one form or another, and most of the time without realizing how much harm we are doing to ourselves. In this insane attitude, we may not feel the pain we inflict on others, but, sooner or later, we certainly feel the pain we inflicted on ourselves. We allow the enemy within to enslave us. Can we use the war within to achieve peace? Yes, we can and we must.

It is important to remember that as long as we are on earth and in this body form, most of us cannot get rid of emotions; however, we can learn to handle them. Anger, fear, hate, and guilt are all part of our so called human condition, which sometimes leads us to become anything but human. The big question is why? The more we insist on projecting our problems, the more we forget to look within, to try and understand who we are, and, above all, to remember love.

Most of our relationships give us a chance to fear, to hate, to get angry, and to love-in other words, to reverse our feelings. Even the most loving relation-ship, let's say with a partner or with a parent, has its moments of love and also despair. This is the ongoing dance of life. This is a difficult dance for many of us. This is the war and peace within us.

I can of my own self do nothing.

John 5:30

We need help, perhaps more often than we realize. We are not able to understand ourselves fully, and even if we try, the ego will interfere and completely misguide us. Only our higher self is able to guide and understand us. It sees the whole picture; it knows exactly what each individual's mission is, where we started, and where we are heading. In short, the higher self has the script of our lives, of the universe, and of the planet.

Only after many sessions of meditation and relaxation exercises and always asking for help from my higher self was I able to let go of the potatoes in my mind.

Today, I look back at my experience and I thank the teenagers for the chance they gave me to find peace again. I thought my job as a volunteer was to help them, but I ended up helping myself too.

Free Will and Free Willie

Man proposes, but God disposes.

Thomas A. Kempis

It was winter in New York. I was working for a major corporation on Wall Street when I found it necessary to take a week off. I went to the Virgin Islands to swim in the warm water of the Caribbean Sea.

I choose to stay in a small, quiet, and inexpensive hotel by the ocean away from the crowds and shopping areas. My room was on the first floor, just a few feet away from the waves. There was a restaurant right by my room, which was very convenient. I could eat, sleep, and swim all day without having to travel. I also thought that the chances to meet any-one I knew in that environment were none. There would be no one to bother me, and certainly no Wall Street executives would come to the hotel.

As soon as I arrived, I dropped my suitcase some-where in my room, dropped my winter clothes, put on my bathing suit, and rushed to the restaurant. I was free, at last.

The greatest power God gave us is the power to choose. We have the opportunity to choose whether we are going to act or procrastinate, believe or doubt, pray or curse, help or heal. We also choose whether we are going to be happy or whether we're going to be sad.

Lou Holtz, 1989

For me, one of the greatest earthly pleasures is to have a good meal in a restaurant by the ocean. This is exactly what was happening. As I was savoring a shrimp cocktail and anxiously waiting for the broiled lobster, I noticed a man and a woman arrive and sit at the bar. I was so involved with my meal that I did not look at them, but somehow, I noticed the man was persistently looking at me. When I decided to look at them, I gave them a smile and went back to eating my shrimp.

It took me a while to realize that I knew the man.

But, by that time, he got up from his seat, came around, sat next to me, shook my hand, and said, nervously, "Odete, I never expected to meet you here. As a matter of fact, I told my friend not to worry; I was choosing a hotel where I was sure I would meet no one I knew."

"Well, well, Willie," I said, "I'm surprised to meet you here, too."

Since I was not sure if his female companion knew he was married, I communicated with him psychically, "Willie, Willie, what are you doing with your life? This is not your wife."

Almost instantly, he introduced me to his female companion who was also very nervous.

"I'm having lots of problems with my marriage, said Willie. "My Wall Street job is a mess. But I'm free to choose and ready to make changes. I really needed a break. My family knows nothing about my whereabouts. Please, Odete, don't tell my wife. If you do, you will cause great problems in our family."

Willie did not have to worry about our encounter. I told him I had not spoken to his wife for a long time and had no intention of calling her.

Take away free will and there remains nothing to be saved.... Salvation is given by God alone, and it is given only to free-will; even as it can-not be wrought without the consent of the receiver it cannot be wrought without the grace of the giver.

St. Bernard, Treatise Concerning Grace and Free Will, c. 1128

Classic Indian teachings mention that our lives are 75 percent predetermined by our past, and 25 percent free will. The thought of predetermination makes a lot of people angry and uncomfortable. They think that God has completely taken over their lives. They find it hard to take responsibility for their actions-past, present, and future. All errors we made in the past can be corrected now. This is why we are endowed with free will which leads to salvation.

If we do not use our free will, the past will continue to rule us. We may not even be aware of the damage we are doing to ourselves. Plato, in the Republic, Book X (620) refers to each soul passing "without looking back under the Throne of Necessity." Apparently, it is necessary for all of us to come to earth to correct something.

What could it be that needs correction beside hate, fear, or anger towards our neighbors, family friends, and enemies? What could it be that everyone fears, but most of us do not have the courage to face?

Could it be that the more we think civilization advances, the more we try to run away from the thought of God-a unified energy that exists within all of us? Could it be that it is necessary for us to come to earth in order to learn to return, and there-fore save ourselves?

Even our journey here is our choice. God is gentle; He endows us with free will to choose. Willie like all of us, was aware of his power to choose, but he was not aware of the real reasons or the necessity to choose. This is the great mystery of life on this planet. This is also what makes life interesting.

All of us try to run away in order to find our way We are in need of correcting something, but we do not know what. We are all in need of going some-where but we do not know exactly where.

I found out, years later, that Willie never separated from his wife and was apparently still married to her. It is true, then, "that man proposes, but God disposes."

Willie and I will always wonder about our encounter. It was our choice to go to the Virgin Islands, Was it our choice to meet? And, if so, why? The mystery of life goes on.

This Bible quote is a reminder of our age of innocence. Nakedness is a symbol of purity. We wear no masks and use no devices to disguise our true self.

At the beginning, Adam and Eve knew nothing yet about suffering. Although they were already on earth in the physical form, their thought system had not yet been corrupted by the fruit of the tree of knowledge of good and evil. But soon, they were tempted and ate the forbidden fruit. Then they started on their journey of joy and pain.

Adam and Eve were told by God that if they ate the forbidden fruit they would surely die. The ser-pent, on the other hand, told them, "Ye shall not surely die." These two conflicting statements remind all of us of our first state of confusion. Indeed, Adam and Eve eventually died. They disposed of their physical body, but not right away.

What was God referring to when He said, "you shall surely die" (Genesis 2:17)? Dying is a metaphor for losing our innocence and forgetting our relationship with our Father.

Then, we choose to go through the self-inflicted pain of remembering. Eating the fruit of the tree of knowledge was our first choice to forget and it still is. As a matter of fact, our whole life is a choice to forget or to remember.

Adam was put to sleep by God; nowhere in the Bible does it say he woke up. Adam is still sleeping, and so are all of us. How could any truly awakened individual continuously choose to eat the forbidden fruit?

What about the tree of life? What kind of life was God referring to? Eternal life the life of the awakened, which has nothing to do with the life or death of the physical body.

Are all of us eating from this tree? Apparently not. When we eat from the tree of life, we'll lose our mask, regain our innocence, and awake. The thoughts of our short life in physical form are replaced by the thoughts of eternal life. This is what the life of Jesus portrays. He never lost his innocence. He always remembered his relationship with his Father. He came to earth to help us remember.

The Passion of the Christ in USA and in Europe

Why are people interested in camouflaging the truth about eternal life? Why is the movie The Passion of the Christ edited in the United States (at least in New York City) to the point of eliminating the last scene the Resurrection?

The Passion that I saw in Europe is more complete and fair. It shows Jesus disrobed and in contemplation near his burial site. His shroud is wrinkled, but it is empty since he is not wearing it. He laid aside his outer garment. His mission on earth was beautifully accomplished. His eternal life will never end, and neither does ours.

Our present civilization leaves much to be desired. Hate is floating around in great proportions and in many forms. Slavery is prominent in many countries. Women and children are the ones that suffer most.

The education implemented in most countries is useless; getting a college degree may do nothing to help people inwardly.

The present generation is spoiled, apathetic, neurotic, and superficial. It is hard to accept that these people will be the leaders in the future. You try to bring up the subject of God or science, and they run away at a speed faster than light.

Our advances in science are leading us outwardly instead of inwardly. Anything from cellular phones (in some countries called mobile) to CDs to Moon and Mars landings could be used to help us reflect on who we are and how life functions on earth and beyond. Our media could be used to bombard us with interesting, detailed information to make us think, ponder, and contemplate.

Eating the forbidden fruit is our way to hide from God-a scapegoat. "Adam and his wife hid themselves from the presence of Lord God amongst the trees of the garden" (Genesis 3:8). Nothing has changed since then. To go on chewing the forbidden fruit does not lead us anywhere, but keeps our digestive system in trouble and wrecks our mind. Then we complain of sickness and blame God. For most people, this is the only time they think of God. They may remember Him, but only to blame Him.

Obviously, most of us continue to eat abundantly from the tree of knowledge of good and evil in the hope of becoming wise (Genesis 3:6). But, who is the wisest? The one who beats up Jesus, or Jesus who says, "You have no power over me. I and my Father are one?"

It is up to us, individuals, to remember that there is also the fruit of the tree of life. Indeed, we are alone and free to choose once again.

Adam Is Still Sleeping

The story of creation is described in Genesis, the first book of the Bible. Besides creating heaven and earth, God also created a man out of the dust of the ground. But the man was lifeless until God gave him the breath of life that is, His Spirit. God called him Adam, and as described in Genesis 2:21 "caused a deep sleep to fall upon Adam, and he slept." Then, He took one of the man's ribs and made a woman. He named her Eve. Now, in the year 2004, we can say that this is also the story of the first transplant of DNA.

It looks like God gave Adam such a strong over-dose of anesthesia that nowhere in the Bible does it say he woke up. Since we are all Adam's descendants, it is logical to assume that mankind has been sleeping since then.

Like Adam, we do not remember that spirit has been implanted in us in the form of the breath of life. Like Adam, we are dreaming a dream structured by a higher intelligence which the Bible calls God. In this dream, Adam's first sentence after he sees Eve must have been, "At last." He felt lonely and realized he needed another body to complement him. He focused on his body, instead of his spirit, in other words, he looked outward instead of inward. And so was the beginning of mankind's dream on earth.

A relationship between Adam and Eve started. Sex and conflict followed. Many eons went by, and conflicts never stopped. The earth is full of people trying to destroy the human spirit. By the time Moses got involved in the Exodus, about 1,140 BC, there were two million people that followed him out of slavery in Egypt through the Sinai Desert on their journey back to Canaan, later known as Israel.

Why did God choose to keep these people in a desert for forty years? Why didn't he choose a tropical forest with plenty of water, trees, fruit, birds, animals, and good shade? The scenario God chose was the best for us to grow and wake-up-a process that is still going on. It is when our needs really hurt us that we give in, and hopefully start to awake. The Egyptian king, known as Pharaoh, endured many plagues which devastated his country and his people, but he still did not allow the Jewish slaves to go free.

It was only when his first born son was killed that he finally let them go. The Pharaoh played games with God unaware that God was testing his faith and his willingness to change and awake. In Exodus 7:3, God says, "And I will harden Pharaoh's heart and multiply my signs and my wonders in the land of Egypt." Obviously, this higher intelligence is our cause and is in command.

There is no water in the desert. People protested and complained to Moses. They wanted to go back to slavery. God told Moses to strike a rock with his rod, and water appeared. Then, they complained about lack of food; God sent them manna, a sub-stance to make food with, and quails. While God took care of them, He also gave them laws to live by. The desert then is nothing but a symbol of the emptiness inside ourselves which can easily be replaced with great fruits when we allow spirit to help us.

As the preparations for their journey to Canaan were going on, Moses begged God to come with them. But God said that he could not go because He'd kill them since they had misbehaved, that is, sinned.

This great energy, this great intelligence that we call God knows that He is always within us in the form of spirit; but God also knows that, at that time, people were not ready, and most of us today are still not ready to understand life this way. So, He came down to our level and told Moses that He was sending an Angel with them to protect them and keep them company. God also knows that we cannot destroy spirit; therefore, there is no death. What happens at the moment we call death is that spirit goes on to another journey, while the physical body seems to enter into a deep sleep, but, like we were told when Adam was created, it is lifeless as the breath of life has gone. We do not need a body to be spirit, but we need spirit to help us play the role of a dreamer and awaken.

During those forty years in the Sinai Desert, and in spite of people's misunderstandings, God never stopped sending them miracles to help them wake up to His great energy, recognize His power, and be stimulated enough to ask for His help.

His miracles have gone as far as sending us another image of himself in the form of a physical body known as Jesus Christ; but that was about 1,500 years after Exodus.

As we choose to allow our dream to go on, God continues to protect us. His love for us is always going on, and so is His smile, as He watches us, even when we misbehave.

Kings and Donkeys

God uses interesting symbols to help us understand his powers and our weakness. For example, in most cultures, a donkey is considered a stubborn and stupid animal. In the English language, a donkey is also called an ass.

Around 1,050 BC, Israel had been ruled for centuries by Judges individuals that prophesied and were in constant communication with the Spirit of the Lord. The Jews decided it was time to imitate the neighbors and enemies, the Philistines, and they looked forward to being ruled by a king.

God, being the ultimate ruler, choose the most handsome, yet weak and stubborn, young man in Israel, Saul, to be their first king. Samuel, the last Judge of Israel, was given the task of locating Saul and anointing him.

What was Saul doing when Samuel met him? He was searching for his father's donkeys that had dis-appeared. Since he could not find them, his servant took him to a prophet for help. That prophet was Samuel who told him that the donkeys had been found and that he would be the first king of Israel.

"Why are you talking to me like that?" asked Saul, "I'm from the smallest tribe of Israel, and of the least important families in the tribe." He felt inferior, and without confidence. When Samuel announced to the people of Israel that they had a king, Saul was "hiding among the luggage" (1 Samuel 10:23).

In his searching for donkeys, he was really searching for himself. As Saul became king, he was sur-rounded by far more donkeys than he could imagine. All sorts of donkeys came to him disguised as priests, governors, military leaders, and so forth. But he did not understand what was happening around him. He proceeded without faith in God. In the end, he went insane. He wanted to kill everyone. He killed eighty-five priests, their families, and animals; he won some battles but lost many more. Saul's story is a mirror of our stubbornness.

In the Bible, there is another story in which a donkey saved the life of a man. A Philistine king asked a sorcerer, Balaam, to go and curse the Jews. But Balaam did not go far because his donkey saw an angel and blocked his way three times, and three times Balaam beat him up. Then, God gave the don-key the ability to speak.

"What have I done to you that deserves your beating me three times?" it asked Balaam.

"You have me look like a fool." Balaam shouted (Numbers 22:28-30).

Then, the angel with a sword a symbol of power-showed himself up to Balaam, who bowed his head, and fell flat on his face. The angel told him that the donkey had saved his life because he was going to kill him.

If, instead of beating his donkey he had asked for God's help when he saw the animal blocking his way, God would have helped him understand his relationship with all living things including his don-key. Beating up the donkey was like beating himself up. We all do this to ourselves in different forms. In the end, Balaam blessed the Jews.

The people of Israel learned a great lesson-kings do not solve a nation's problems. Saul's death was the death of an ideal. The problem with mankind was, and still is, not in the form of the governments, but in our ways of thinking. Our stubbornness to think that we can do better by ourselves without asking for God's guidance is our basic problem. Indeed, we are like donkeys, stubborn and ignorant. Just like Saul, most of us do not have the courage to look within and recognize our weakness.

Saul faced life as he faced death, without asking for God's help. He was not able to discern the stubbornness within himself, and like most of us, he didn't even try. He'd rather throw himself on the top of his sword and end his life than ask for God's help. No wonder God chose him to be the first king of Israel, for this is an interesting way to find out that men can be as stubborn as donkeys, but not all don-keys are as stubborn as men, as we saw in the example of Balaam's donkey. He listened to the angel, was even able to speak and saved Balaam's life.

We, the Vagabonds.

A vagabond is an individual who wanders in a haze from place to place. We are all vagabonds as we dream of running away from our source, our true home. After Adam and Eve's son, Cain, killed his brother, Abel, God said to Cain,

> So now you are cursed from the earth...when you till
> the ground, it shall no longer yield its strength to you. A
> fugitive and a vagabond you shall be on the earth.
>
> Genesis 4:12

Earth became a vagabond-land.

When I was a volunteer at Covenant House, an institution for runaway teenagers, I telephoned many parents to let them know where their children were. Most of the parents did not care. Some did not answer the phone call. They not only let their children run away, they too were running away from their children.

Indeed, our wandering state reflects in everything we do, but we do not realize what is happening. The Bible has many examples of runaways; it is the story of vagabonds. In Philemon, a chapter in the New Testament, Onesimus is a slave who ran away from his master. It was Apostle Paul's task to convince both to reconcile.

In the Old Testament, the story of the twin brothers, Esau and Jacob, is a great symbol of a fugitive and a vagabond and his return home. They were Abraham's grandchildren. Esau, having been born first, sold his birthright to Jacob in exchange for a bowl of soup; later he wanted to kill Jacob.

Forced to run away, Jacob was a fugitive for many years, until God said to him, "Return to the land of your father and grandfather, and to your relatives there, and I will be with you." Genesis 31:3

Even so, Jacob was afraid of meeting his brother. He made all kinds of preparations, and when he saw his brother approaching, he placed his wives and children in front of him for protection. But God is the real and only protector: He makes all the necessary arrangements. So "Esau ran to meet him, and embraced him...and kissed him, and they wept" (Genesis 33:4, 5).

Since we are all afraid to be punished when we go back home, this great story in the Bible should make us ponder and realize that there is nothing to fear. Our protector arranges everything in advance; as a matter of fact, everything was arranged before the world began. Indeed, all we need is faith in the energy that exists within us and prepares for us the best outcome possible.

We, the vagabonds, are predestined home in peace and in love, but only if we have faith and ask for help. to go back home in peace and in love, but only if we have faith and ask for help.

Reversing the Blame Game

For most of us, reversing simply means seeing the other side of the coin. In the Bible, reversing means going back to our original unified state of mind. We may think that we can see the other side of the coin by ourselves. But true reversing can only be achieved by a higher energy and intelligence, which is beyond our understanding. In the Old Testament, this energy is called God, and in the New Testament it is called the Holy Spirit; we all know they are the same.

> I will once again astonish these hypocrites with amazing
> wonders. The wisdom of the wise will pass away, and
> the intelligence of the intelligent will disappear.
>
> Isaiah 29:14

It should not be surprising that Albert Einstein, a man known as having a superior intelligence, once wrote, "We should never lose a holy curiosity." For Einstein, a very important state was what he called "an oceanic feeling." He knew that something invisible and extraordinary controlled us.

> God has made the wisdom of this world look foolish... He saw to
> it that the world would never know him through human wisdom,
> he has used our foolish preaching to save those who believe.
>
> Corinthians 1:20

How can this be done? We have been told that nothing is impossible for God. In the meantime, we wonder about his activities. We do not want to accept that we are responsible for our actions. We prefer to blame others for our present human condition. We blame the barbarian invasions, the Crusades, Napoleon, the World Wars of the last century, family members, co-workers, and so forth. Above all, and most important, we blame our par-ents. We don't understand that we can correct our mistakes, otherwise called sins.

The unpleasant thoughts and actions imposed on us by others and by ourselves, including pain, can be reversed, for God, as read in the following quote: It pleased God through the foolishness of the message preached to save those who believe (1 Corinthians 1:21).

Life on earth is structured in such a way that we have to go through certain ordeals, even painful ones, to correct our thoughts and end our illusion of separation from God. This has been written many times, but most of us still do not get it.

During an encounter with a blind man, the disciples asked Jesus,

"Master, who did sin, this man or his
parents, that he was born blind?"
Jesus answered, "Neither this man nor his parents have sinned, but this happened so that the
work of God might be displayed in his life."

John 9:2,3

Over one thousand years before Christ, the prophet Ezekiel (18:20) wrote,

"What?" you ask: "Doesn't the child pay for the
parent's sins?"

No. For if the child does what is just and right and keeps my Decrees, that child will surely live.

These are excellent examples of the importance of stopping our blame game, and taking action to heal by cooperating with our higher self, the source of our unified state of mind. This is the only way the works of God can be manifested. Since we allowed the erroneous thought of separation from our source to be introduced in our minds, it is only through us-individuals and sometimes as a collective-that they can be reversed.

Let's look unto ourselves and ask for His help so that we go back to our original state of mind where we are one with Him.

Shiva and the Dance of Life

What does not kill me makes me stronger.

Friedrich Nietzche

My friend, Mary, is having a hard time trying to reconcile the good, the bad, and the ugly the dance of life.

Mary has everything most women want in life-a summer home,

a townhouse, cars, children, grand-children, lots of good food, and a husband.

But Mary's husband has had several strokes, her children bother her, and she is suffering from serious depression. Recently, she had to take care of her grandchildren because her daughter, who is also married and has everything most women want in life, decided she needed a rest. Mary's husband had another stroke while she was taking care of their grandchildren.

I called her daughter and suggested to her not to send her children again to her parents due to their health condition. She agreed and promised never to do that again. After talking to me, she went downstairs, fell down, and broke her foot. The children were sent back to the grandparents but, this time, they also took their pets with them.

Nothing happens to anybody which he is not fitted by nature to bear.
Marcus Aurelius AD121-80: Meditations

Throughout history we have tried to discover who we really are. Now, we are just beginning to under-stand the dance of life. All events in our lives are programmed to lead us to correct our erroneous thoughts. Everyone we meet, every path we follow, gives us a chance to look within if we choose to do so.

In the midst of our encounters, most of us forget to appreciate the chance we have to learn and grow. We focus mostly on the negative, which is what I did when I telephoned my friend's daughter.

If A is a success in life, then A equals x plus y plus z.
Work is x, y is play, and z is keeping your mouth shut.
Albert Einstein

By focusing only on the negative, I felt pity and sorrow for Mary and her husband. Such feelings of compassion did not allow me to go beyond the negative. This way of thinking may seem cruel. I'm not saying that we should not help each other. What I'm saying is that there is always a limit as to how much we can do for others; there is a higher self in charge of helping everyone follow their path.

Tragedy might really to be a great kick at misery.

D.H. Lawrence

Life is full of contradictions; war and peace, love and hate. Life is a constant dance between light and darkness.

They that sow in tears: shall reap in joy.

Psalm 126:5

A great figure in the dance of life is the Hindu god Shiva. Although his name literarily means the kind and the friendly one, he has three faces and combines in himself contradictory qualities of both destroyer and restorer.

What does Shiva destroy? Ignorance. This is considered a great blessing in Hindu culture. Indeed, what better accomplishment could there be during our short visit on earth than to learn to destroy the erroneous concept we have of ourselves?

How can we destroy such ignorance, in other words, how can we work towards our salvation? The Hindu culture teaches the use of yoga and meditation. Other cultures teach prayers. More primitive cultures teach sacrifice. Whichever path we chose, we must always act and react, even the Bible says that. We cannot and must not isolate ourselves completely, and even if we try, our thoughts will always be in charge of our lives, and we have to learn to handle them. So, there is a constant physical and mental movement going on a dance. How ugly or beautiful we make that dance is up to us.

If we are successful, we begin to understand and appreciate the dance of life. We'll move along in a soft way. The negative can destroy us or it can help restore our sanity; that is, if we learn to dance around it, even flirt with it so that we attract the negativity close enough to allow the light to illuminate our minds, and wipe out our ignorance about our true self.

Bibliography

Barnett, Lincoln. The Universe and Dr. Einstein. New York: William Sloane Associates Publishers. Revised Edition, 1950.

Bigote, Odete Martins. You Can Remember Love: Contemplations on Science and Spirituality. Bloomington, IN.: 1st Books Library, 2000, Bohm, David. Wholeness and the Implicate Order. London and New York: Routledge and Kegan Paul Ltd., and Methuen, Inc., 1980.

Bohm, David, and David Peat. Science, Order and Creativity. New York: Bantam Books, 1987.

Calder, Nigel. Einstein's Universe. New York: Viking Press, 1979.

Hawking, Stephen W. A Brief History of Time, From the big bang to Black Holes. New York: Bantam, 1988.

Hawking, Stephen W. and Leonard Mlodinow. The

Grand Design. New York: Bantam Books, 2010. Jeans, Sir James. The Mysterious Universe. New York: The MacMillan Company, 1932.

Kant, Immanuel. Critic of Pure Reason. New York: Random House, 1947.

Kant, Immanuel. Man and Spirit: The Speculative Philosophers. New York: Random House, 1947. Lovejoy, Arthur O. The Great Chain of Being. Cambridge: Harvard University press, 1936.

Nilsson, Lennart. A Child Is Born. New York: Dell Publishing, 1993.

Pessoa, Fernando. Selected Poems (translated by Jonathan Griffin) (2nd Edition). London: Penguin Books, Ltd., 1974.

Plato. The Great Dialogues of Plato. New York: Mentor Books, The American Library of World Literature, Inc., 1956.

Webster's Third New International Dictionary. 1961.

Webster's Third New International Dictionary. Copyright 1981 by Merriam-Webster Inc. Whitman, Walt. Leaves of Grass. New York: Penguin, 1995.

Wolf, Fred Allen. Parallel Universes. The Search for Other Worlds. New York: Simon & Schuster, 1988

Wolf, Fred Allen. Time Loops and Space Twists: How God Created the Universe. San Antonio, TX: Hierophant Publishers, 2011.

Endnotes

1 Stephen W. Hawking, A Brief History of Time, From the big bang to Black Holes (New York: Bantam, 1988), 175.

2 Ibid.

3 Stephen W. Hawking and Leonard Mlodinow, The Grand Design (New York: Bantam Books, 2010), 18.

4 Ibid., 83.

5 Ibid., 51.

6 Ibid., 172.

7 Ibid., 173.

8 Ibid., 46.

9 Ibid., 34.

10 Lincoln Barnett, The Universe and Dr. Einstein (New York: William Sloane Associates Publishers. Revised Edition, 1950), 21.

11 Hawking and Mlodinow, 34.

12 Ibid., 172.

13 Ibid., 53.

14 Fernando Pessoa, Selected Poems (translated by Jonathan Griffin) (2nd Edition) (London: Penguin Books, Ltd., 1974), 10.

15 Lennart Nilsson, A Child Is Born (New York: Dell Publishing, 1993), 56.

16 Ibid., 12.

17 Ibid., 41.

18 Ibid., 66.

19 Ibid.

20 Ibid., 80.

21 Ibid., 107.

22 Ibid., 112.

23 Hawking and Mlodinow, 5.

24 Sir James Jeans, The Mysterious Universe (New York: The MacMillan Company, 1932), 186.

25 Ibid., 182.

26 Barnett, 127.

27 David Bohm, Wholeness and the Implicate Order (London and New York: Routledge and Kegan Paul Ltd., and Methuen, Inc., 1980), 209.

28 Bohm, 49.

29 Nigel Calder, Einstein's Universe (New York: Viking Press, 1979), 17.

30 Ibid., 13.

31 Calder, 123.

32 Hawking, 126. 33 Ibid., 175.

34 Ibid., 165.

35 Hawking and Mlodinow, 180.

36 Fred Allen Wolf, Time Loops and Space Twists: How God Created the Universe (San Antonio, TX: Hierophant Publishers, 2011), 122.

37 Webster's Third New International Dictionary (1961), 107.

38 Immanuel Kant, Man and Spirit: The Speculative Philosophers (New York: Random House, 1947), 424.

39 Hawking and Mlodinow, 180-181.

www.ingramcontent.com/pod-product-compliance
Lightning Source LLC
Chambersburg PA
CBHW041626140626
46547CB00030B/1101